THE FLORIDA POSTCONVICTION JOURNAL

volumes 1 & 2
spring 2010 - spring 2013

a quarterly publication of

Loren Rhoton, P.A.

Loren Rhoton
Ryan Sydejko

The Florida Postconviction Journal
A publication of Loren Rhoton, P.A.
© 2010 – 2013 Loren Rhoton and Ryan Sydejko

In an effort to help indigent Florida inmates, Loren Rhoton and Ryan Sydejko, of the Law Office of Loren Rhoton, P.A., previously contributed legal self-help articles to the original Florida Prison Legal Perspectives. When FPLP ceased publishing in 2010, Mr. Rhoton and Mr. Sydejko continued providing inmates with helpful postconviction legal advice through a new newsletter, The Florida Postconviction Journal. The Florida Postconviction Journal is published by Loren Rhoton, P.A., on a quarterly basis and is provided free of charge to Florida prisoners. This collection contains the first seven issues of The Florida Postconviction Journal.

Contact Loren Rhoton, P.A., at:
412 E. Madison Street
Suite 1111
Tampa, Florida 33602

lorenrhoton@rhotonpostconviction.com
rhotonpostconviction.com

The Florida Postconviction Journal

Volume 1
Issue 1

a quarterly publication of Loren Rhoton, P.A.

Spring 2010

Florida Prison Legal Perspectives Update

by Loren D. Rhoton

In 1999, I had the opportunity and pleasure to become acquainted with the Florida Prisoner's Legal Aid Organization, Inc. (FPLAO) and its newspaper, the Florida Prison Legal Perspectives (FPLP). At that time, I was greatly impressed with the efforts of the FPLAO founder, Bobby Posey, and his wife Teresa. From inside prison, with the assistance of Teresa, Bobby managed to run an organization that zealously advocated for inmates and their families. Through FPLAO and FPLP, Bobby and Teresa tirelessly fought for the rights of inmates and their loved ones. I admired Bobby for his efforts, and, consequently, offered my services to the non-profit FPLAO group in the form of providing _pro bono_ legal advice to the organization and submitting articles for an ongoing legal self-help column (_Post Conviction Corner_) in FPLP.

Through the years, I became friends with Bobby and Teresa and my respect for them and their efforts only continued to grow. It is with great sadness now that I write that Bobby Posey passed away near the end of 2009. All Florida inmates were certainly better off for having Bobby Posey on their side. Without a doubt, Bobby Posey will be missed by many.

With Bobby's passing, both FPLAO and FPLP have ceased to exist. Without question, the absence of FPLAO will leave a great void for its many members who counted on the FPLP for the advocacy, news and advice that were relevant and meaningful to inmates. My office, Loren Rhoton, P.A., will be attempting, in its own small way, to carry on the spirit of FPLAO with a quarterly newsletter dedicated to prisoners' interests. As the main focus of my office is criminal appeals and postconviction issues, the content of my newsletter will consist mainly of self-help legal articles (much like the _Post Conviction Corner_ articles that I regularly published in FPLP). The newsletter, as it develops, will also likely contain case law updates and perhaps helpful articles from inmate contributors. I know that this newsletter will not be as varied or in-depth as FPLP, and I can only hope that my efforts will be helpful to the people who previously relied on FPLP for advice and information.

This premier issue is dedicated to Bobby Posey.

Lone Opportunity to Amend Postconviction Claims Pursuant to _Spera v. State_

As many postconviction litigants are likely aware, _Spera v. State_, 971 So.2d 754 (Fla. 2007), provides the opportunity to amend claims found facially insufficient by the trial court. Many courts have dealt with the extent to which the ability to amend must be made available. For instance, the First DCA has held that a single opportunity to amend is adequate. _Nelson v. State_, 977 So.2d 710 (Fla. 1st DCA 2008). But, what if the movant does not timely act on that opportunity?

In _Williams v. State_, 35 Fla. L. Weekly D100, the First DCA answered that question. In _Williams_, the defendant filed a _pro se_ twenty-issue Rule 3.850 Motion for Postconviction Relief. The court summarily denied most claims, but granted an evidentiary hearing on others. The defendant subsequently obtained counsel whom filed a motion to amend the summarily denied claims pursuant to _Spera_. An evidentiary hearing was held, and the court ruled on the claims from the evidentiary hearing, before counsel had amended the facially insufficient claims.

The First DCA ruled that because counsel was given the opportunity to amend, of which he chose not to act, _Spera_ was satisfied and any claim he may have had under _Spera_ was deemed waived.

The importance of the Court's holding in this case is that _Spera_ only requires a single _opportunity_ to amend. In the event the postconviction litigant chooses not to, or fails to, act during that window of opportunity, any _Spera_ claim may be waived.

About Loren Rhoton, P.A.

Loren Rhoton, P.A. is a law firm that focuses exclusively on postconviction actions and inmate issues. The mission of Loren Rhoton, P.A. is to ensure that justice is accomplished in each and every case the firm undertakes. The firm's area of practice ranges from direct criminal appeals and postconviction actions to assisting inmates in dealing with the Florida Department of Corrections. Loren Rhoton, P.A., is a small firm, consisting of Mr. Loren D. Rhoton and Mr. Ryan J. Sydejko. The firm strives to keep a small caseload in order to give each case the individual attention it deserves. We are not a volume business. We do not accept every case that is presented to the firm for representation. A thorough review of any potential case will be conducted before the firm undertakes full representation. If you wish to have your case reviewed for representation, please contact Loren Rhoton for more information. If inquiring about representation, please do not send any materials to the firm that you wish to have returned to you.

Loren D. Rhoton, Esq.

Loren D. Rhoton is an attorney in private practice with the law office of Loren Rhoton, P.A., in Tampa, Florida. Mr. Rhoton graduated from the University of Toledo College of Law and has been a member in good standing with The Florida Bar since his admission to practice in 1995. The exclusive focus of Mr. Rhoton's practice is dedicated to assisting Florida inmates with their criminal appeal/postconviction cases.

Mr. Rhoton is a member of The Florida Bar's Appellate Division. He is also a member of the U.S. District Court, in and for the Middle and Northern Districts of Florida. Mr. Rhoton is licensed to practice before the U.S. Court of Appeals for the 11th Circuit and is also certified to practice before the U.S. Supreme Court. Mr. Rhoton regularly practices before Federal District Courts and the U.S. Court of Appeals for the 11th Circuit.

Mr. Rhoton typically deals with clients who have lengthy prison sentences. Mr. Rhoton has investigated and pursued hundreds of postconviction cases. He has practiced in all phases of the Florida Judicial System, all the way from misdemeanor county courts up to the Florida Supreme Court. Additionally, Mr. Rhoton has been directly responsible for amendments to Florida Rule of Criminal Procedure 3.850 (the main vehicle for most postconviction actions). Mr. Rhoton is appointed by the Florida Supreme Court to the Florida Criminal Rules Steering Committee, Subcommittee on Postconviction Relief, which is focused on rewriting Florida Rule of Criminal Procedure 3.850. Mr. Rhoton works on said subcommittee with judges and other governmental officials in an effort to improve the administration and execution of postconviction proceedings. Mr. Rhoton's role on said committee has been to advocate for changes that will be beneficial to postconviction litigants (inmates).

For over a decade, Mr. Rhoton authored a bimonthly article, *Post Conviction Corner*, for Florida Prison Legal Perspectives. Selected articles from *Post Conviction Corner* have been compiled and printed in a legal self-help book, *Postconviction Relief for the Florida Prisoner*. Mr. Rhoton also served on the Board of Directors of the Florida Prisoner's Legal Aid Organization, Inc.

Ryan J. Sydejko, Esq.

Ryan J. Sydejko is an attorney with the law office of Loren Rhoton, P.A. His practice focuses primarily on postconviction matters for those incarcerated throughout the State of Florida. He has argued cases before many circuit courts and District Courts of Appeal and has several published opinions. Mr. Sydejko has also presented cases to the Supreme Court of Florida and the U.S. District Courts for the Middle and Northern Districts of Florida.

Mr. Sydejko graduated from the University of Minnesota with a degree in political science and attended the University of Tulsa College of Law. As a student, he authored a law review article entitled: "International Influence on Democracy: How Terrorism Exploited a Deteriorating Fourth Amendment." The article, exploring how domestic terrorist threats have reshaped everyday law enforcement procedures, was published in the Spring 2006 edition of the Wayne State University Law School Journal of Law in Society. Mr. Sydejko also wrote articles for the Florida Prison Legal Perspectives. Mr. Sydejko is a member in good standing with the Florida Bar and is qualified to practice in all Florida state courts, as well as the Federal District Courts for the Middle and Northern Districts of Florida.

The Florida Postconviction Journal

Volume 1
Issue 1

a quarterly publication of Loren Rhoton, P.A.

page 2 of 6

Notable Firm Cases

Dames v. State, 773 So.2d 563 (Fla. 2d DCA 2000) – Improper summary denial of Rule 3.850 Motion reversed & remanded for evidentiary hearing.

Dames v. State, 807 So.2d 756 (Fla. 2d DCA 2002) – First Degree Murder conviction vacated & new trial granted due to ineffective counsel

Battle v. State, 710 So.2d 628 (Fla. 2d DCA 1998) – Improper Habitual Felony Offender Sentence on violation of probation reversed & remanded for resentencing

Mitchell v. State, 734 So.2d 1067 (Fla. 1st DCA 1999) - counsel can render ineffective assistance for failure to argue boarded-up structure is not a 'dwelling' under arson statute

Caban v. State, 9 So.3d 50 (Fla. 5th DCA 2009) – counsel can be ineffective for failing to object to improper impeachment of defense expert witnesses in Shaken Baby Syndrome case

Graff v. State, 846 So.2d 582 (Fla. 2d DCA 2003) – attorney's misadvice as to potential sentence can amount to ineffective assistance of counsel sufficient to justify withdrawal of plea.

Easley v. State, 742 So.2d 463 (Fla. 2d DCA 1999) – counsel can render ineffective assistance for failure to investigate insanity defense.

Campbell v. State, 16 So.3d 316 (Fla. 2d DCA 2009) – Manifest Injustice – summary denial of Rule 3.800 motion to correct illegal sentence reversed & remanded on manifest injustice grounds.

Thompson v. State, 987 So.2d 727 (Fla. 4th DCA 2008) – Reversal of Life Sentences – entitled to *de novo* resentencing upon correction of improper consecutive life sentences for murder and burglary.

Williams v. State, 777 So.2d 947 (Fla. 2000) – Right to Belated Postconviction Motion – if post-conviction counsel fails to timely file Rule 3.850 Motion, defendant has right to file belated appeal.

Parker v. State, 977 So.2d 671 (Fla. 4th DCA 2008) – Sentence reversed & remanded for resentencing due to judicial vindictiveness

Second District Court of Appeal Rules on Abandoned Investigative Technique

In it's recent case, *Smith v. State*, 2010 WL 21178, the Second District Court of Appeal (DCA) addressed the use of the FBI's recently abandoned use of comparative bullet lead analysis (CBLA) as newly discovered evidence in postconviction cases.

In thousands of cases, spanning decades of jurisprudence, the FBI used a technique of comparing spent cartridges to unused ammunition to determine whether they were from similar batches. In *Smith*, an FBI special agent offered similar testimony, linking the defendant to homicides in 1989 and 1990. Over two decades later, in a November 2007 joint-investigation by the Washington Post and CBS News' "60" Minutes, a former FBI chief concluded that CBLA could not reliably support the proposition that a particular bullet came from a particular box of ammunition. The research further discovered that the FBI had abandoned this technique several years earlier, in 2004, but had failed to notify anyone as to why a investigatory technique utilized for decades was now suddenly being discontinued.

The defendant in *Smith* had filed a Florida Rule of Criminal Procedure 3.850 Motion for Postconviction Relief alleging that evidence indicated a scientific theory advanced by the State at his trials (in 1989 & 1990) had been recently discredited and abandoned, constituting newly discovered evidence.

The Court, citing its decision in *Clark v. State*, 995 So.2d 1112 (Fla. 2d DCA 2008), reversed the trial court and remanded the defendant's motion for an evidentiary hearing on the newly discovered evidence claim, holding that the defendant "alleged that evidence that CBLA has been discredited and abandoned was unknown at the time of his trials and could not have been discovered by the use of due diligence."

For individuals with offenses pre-dating the FBI's 2004 cessation of the use of CBLA, it may be prudent to review your materials, as well as *Smith* and *Clark*, to determine whether the State offered testimony regarding CBLA, as a potential avenue to seek postconviction relief may have opened.

On the third Friday of each month, Loren Rhoton can be heard discussing postconviction issues that are of interest to prisoners and their families on the radio show *Justice for All*. *Justice for All* is hosted by Pastor Dana Jackson and broadcasts every Friday from 11 a.m. to Noon on WOKB a.m. 1680 out of Orlando, Fla. The radio show can also be heard online at: www.wokbradio.com.

Preservation of the Attorney-Client Privilege While Incarcerated

by Ryan J. Sydejko

A fundamental aspect of legal representation requires that a client be permitted to discuss his legal affairs with his attorney, in private, and with openness and candor. Failing to provide an attorney with all known aspects of one's case, for fear of public dissemination of those communications, could negatively impact the overall representation of a client. Therefore, a client must be provided a forum to discuss his case. Traditional sanctity of the attorney-client privilege emanates from common law, and was later encompassed in the Sixth Amendment to the U.S. Constitution. *See U.S. v. Melvin*, 650 F.2d 641 (5th Cir. 1981).

The Florida legislature has also spoken regarding this privilege, codifying that persons who seek legal advice may have their confidential communications with attorneys protected. *See* Fla. Stat. § 90.502. This allows clients to refuse to disclose, and prevents attorneys from breaching the confidentiality. *Id.* There are several criteria that must be satisfied prior to a proper invocation of the privilege, and it is important that any potential client review the pertinent statute to ensure that all criteria are met. *See id.* This article focuses on one of those criteria, namely that the communication between an attorney and client are confidential only if they exclude unnecessary third parties. Fla. Stat. § 90.502(1)(c).

Preservation of the attorney-client privilege by incarcerated individuals can frequently become rather onerous, especially in light of the requirement that third parties be excluded from the conversation. A communication is only protected by the attorney-client privilege when intended to be confidential and was made under circumstances in which it was reasonably expected to be confidential. *Melvin*, 650 F.2d at 645. Obviously, securing any privacy in order to enjoy a confidential communication is a tall order for those incarcerated in Florida. This is why it is vital for inmates and attorneys alike, to understand and properly invoke their right to speak in private. One way for an inmate to enjoy a privileged attorney-client communication is in-person at the institution. While such face-to-face communication may be ideal, it is rather burdensome. Inmates move frequently, and are rarely housed near their attorneys. Furthermore, such an arrangement places an undue financial burden on inmates, as most attorneys would charge for the time spent traveling to a from a distant institution. These were likely both considerations when the Florida Administrative Code was drafted regarding inmates and telephone use.

Section 33-602.205 of the Florida Administrative Code is entitled "Inmate Telephone Use." In that section, an inmate's telephone privileges are set forth. Applicable to the instant article is subsection (3), which pertains to "Calls to Attorneys." Subsection (3)(a) sets forth that "Inmates *shall* be allowed to make *private* telephone calls to attorneys upon presentation to the warden or his designee of evidence that the call is necessary . . . except as authorized by warrant or order of court, telephone calls to attorneys made pursuant to this section shall *not be monitored* or electronically recorded." *Id.* (emphasis added).

There are several points worthy of further discussion regarding subsection (3)(a), but this article will focus on the privacy mandate. Privacy, as in exclusion of third parties, is of the utmost importance, as an inmate may wish to keep the conversation from the prying ears of prison officials. Herein lies the problem at many institutions. Several institutions set up inmate phone calls in the office of the classification officers. Most often, the classification officer is sitting beside the inmate throughout the call. In such a scenario, the call is not "private" as required by subsection (3)(a), and, further, it waives the attorney-client privilege as a third party is present. This could ultimately permit the classification officer to relay portions of the conversation to supervisors or prosecutors. Institutions are required to designate an area where private calls can occur, without the presence of an officer. Occasionally, this will take some prodding by the attorney, and perhaps a phone call to the warden's office.

Lastly, absent a warrant or other court order, the telephone line cannot be monitored when the legal phone call is set up by the attorney pursuant to subsection (3)(a). Institutions are permitted, however, to monitor phone calls made by inmates from their calling lists. Therefore, it is preferable to schedule phone calls through classifications to ensure the call is on a secured line.

The attorney-client privilege is sacred and emanates from hundreds of years of common law. One should not take it lightly or be forced into unknowingly waiving it. Therefore, inmates, and their attorneys alike, may wish to review the Code in order to ensure their communications are truly private, thereby preserving the attorney-client privilege.

The Florida Postconviction Journal

Volume 1
Issue 1

a quarterly publication of Loren Rhoton, P.A.

page 5 of 6

Miranda: The Right to Remain Silent Versus Actual Silence

One investigative technique of law enforcement officers is to question a suspect numerous times in an attempt to extricate a confession. As many are aware, *Miranda* warnings serve to protect the accused, by informing them of rights they may exercise to prevent undesirable or repetitive questioning. One such right is the right to remain silent.

In *Dyer v. State*, 16 So.3d 990 (Fla. 3d DCA 2009), the Third District Court explained the difference between invocation of the right and practice of the right. In *Dyer*, the defendant "ignored detectives and stared at the wall" during questioning. Eventually, after several attempts at interrogation, the defendant spoke and offered inculpatory statements. The Court held that because the defendant merely practiced the right to remain silent, and did not specifically invoke it, the inculaptory statements were admissible. Because the defendant never invoked his right to remain silent, the Court wrote, he could not avail himself of the protections afforded by the right.

To Subscribe to *The Florida Postconviction Journal*:

Loren Rhoton, P.A.

Postconviction Attorneys

412 East Madison Street
Suite 1111
Tampa, Florida 33602
Tel: 813-226-3138
Fax: 813-221-2182
Email:
lorenrhoton@rhotonpostconviction.com
rsydejko@rhotonpostconviction.com

- Direct Appeals
- Belated Appeals
- Rule 3.850 Motions
- Illegal Sentence Corrections
- Rule 9.141 Petitions
- Federal Habeas Corpus Petitions
- Clemency Petitions and Waivers

The Florida Postconviction Journal publishes up to four times per year. You are receiving this due to your previous subscription or interest with Florida Prison Legal Perspectives. This Journal provides resources for information affecting prisoners, their families, friends, loved ones, and the general public of the State of Florida. Promoting skilled access to the court system for indigent prisoners is a primary goal of this publication. Due to the volume of mail that is received, not all correspondence can be returned. If you would like return of materials, please enclose a postage-paid and pre-addressed envelope. This publication is not meant to be a substitute for legal or other professional advice. The material addressed in the Journal should not be relied upon as authoritative and may not contain sufficient information to deal with specific legal issues.

The Florida Postconviction Journal
a publication of Loren Rhoton, P.A.
412 East Madison Street
Suite 1111
Tampa, FL 33602

CHANGE SERVICE REQUESTED

Name
Institution
Street Address
City, State, Zip

The Florida Postconviction Journal

Volume 1
Issue 2

a quarterly publication of Loren Rhoton, P.A.

Fall 2010

Life Sentence Without Parole Stricken by U.S. Supreme Court as Applied to Juveniles Tried as Adult Offenders

In May of this year, the Supreme Court of the United States ruled that it is unconstitutional for Florida courts to impose a life sentence without the possibility of parole on juvenile offenders who have committed an offense other than homicide. In Graham v. Florida, 130 S.Ct. 2011 (2010), the Supreme Court overturned the decision of First District Court of Appeals of Florida that upheld a life sentence without parole for a defendant who was sixteen years old at the time he committed an armed burglary and attempted armed burglary. The Graham Court held that the Florida sentencing scheme that allowed for a life sentence without the possibility of parole for a non-homicide criminal defendant violated the Eighth Amendment of the U.S. Constitution's prohibition against cruel and unusual punishment. The Supreme Court issued a bright-line rule demarcating the age at which a straight life sentence for a juvenile offender is inappropriate, writing: "This Court now holds that for a juvenile offender who did not commit homicide the Eighth Amendment forbids the sentence of life without parole." Graham at 2030.

Graham did not specifically state that its holding was retroactive. Nevertheless, given the constitutional nature of the issue and the fact that the court established a bright-line rule, there is persuasive argument in favor of retroactivity. Any inmates who received life sentences without the possibility of parole for a non-homicide case that was committed while the defendant was a juvenile would be wise to file a postconviction motion attacking the constitutionality of the sentence as cruel and unusual, in violation of the Eighth and Fourteenth Amendments of the U.S. Constitution. As always, it is recommended that any such collateral attack be filed as soon as possible to avoid the possibility of new case law that could limit the application of the ruling.

Postconviction Hearings and the Defendant's Right (sometimes) to be Present

In McDowell v. State, 25 So.3d 1257 (Fla. 2d DCA 2010), the Second District Court of Appeal acknowledged that a defendant's presence is not always required for postconviction evidentiary hearings pursuant to Rule 3.850. In McDowell, the defendant was not present for his evidentiary hearing because his counsel was unsuccessful in having him transported from federal custody. McDowell, 25 So.3d at 1258. Although counsel objected, the trial court proceeded with the evidentiary hearing anyways. Id. One issue raised by the defendant was premised upon misadvice of trial counsel. Id. The trial court heard testimony from the defendant's trial attorney, and subsequently denied relief on that issue. Id. On appeal, the defendant argued that he had a right to be present and testify as to his recollection of the events. Id.

The Second District Court of Appeal noted that a postconviction movant's presence is not required at every postconviction evidentiary hearing. Id. But, the Court continued, when the defendant has personal knowledge of material facts in dispute (such as what the trial attorney's advice was), the defendant "should" be afforded the opportunity to be present and testify. Id. at 1259. Further, a defendant's presence is necessary to adequately cross-examine witnesses against him. Id.

Ultimately, the Second District Court of Appeal held that the trial court abused its discretion in failing to permit the defendant an opportunity to testify and assist his counsel in cross-examination of witnesses against him. Id. The case was reversed and remanded with instructions for the trial court to conduct a second evidentiary hearing, this time with the defendant present. Id.

About Loren Rhoton, P.A.

Loren Rhoton, P.A. is a law firm that focuses exclusively on postconviction actions and inmate issues. The mission of Loren Rhoton, P.A. is to ensure that justice is accomplished in each and every case the firm undertakes. The firm's area of practice ranges from direct criminal appeals and postconviction actions to assisting inmates in dealing with the Florida Department of Corrections. Loren Rhoton, P.A., is a small firm, consisting of Mr. Loren D. Rhoton and Mr. Ryan J. Sydejko. The firm strives to keep a small caseload in order to give each case the individual attention it deserves. We are not a volume business. We do not accept every case that is presented to the firm for representation. A thorough review of any potential case will be conducted before the firm undertakes full representation. If you wish to have your case reviewed for representation, please contact Loren Rhoton for more information. If inquiring about representation, please do not send any materials to the firm that you wish to have returned to you.

Loren D. Rhoton, Esq.

Loren D. Rhoton is an attorney in private practice with the law office of Loren Rhoton, P.A., in Tampa, Florida. Mr. Rhoton graduated from the University of Toledo College of Law and has been a member in good standing with The Florida Bar since his admission to practice in 1995. The exclusive focus of Mr. Rhoton's practice is dedicated to assisting Florida inmates with their criminal appeal/postconviction cases.

Mr. Rhoton is a member of The Florida Bar's Appellate Division. He is also a member of the U.S. District Court, in and for the Middle and Northern Districts of Florida. Mr. Rhoton is licensed to practice before the U.S. Court of Appeals for the 11th Circuit and is also certified to practice before the U.S. Supreme Court. Mr. Rhoton regularly practices before Federal District Courts and the U.S. Court of Appeals for the 11th Circuit.

Mr. Rhoton typically deals with clients who have lengthy prison sentences. Mr. Rhoton has investigated and pursued hundreds of postconviction cases. He has practiced in all phases of the Florida Judicial System, all the way from misdemeanor county courts up to the Florida Supreme Court. Additionally, Mr. Rhoton has been directly responsible for amendments to Florida Rule of Criminal Procedure 3.850 (the main vehicle for most postconviction actions). Mr. Rhoton is appointed by the Florida Supreme Court to the Florida Criminal Rules Steering Committee, Subcommittee on Postconviction Relief, which is focused on rewriting Florida Rule of Criminal Procedure 3.850. Mr. Rhoton works on said subcommittee with judges and other governmental officials in an effort to improve the administration and execution of postconviction proceedings. Mr. Rhoton's role on said committee has been to advocate for changes that will be beneficial to postconviction litigants (inmates).

For over a decade, Mr. Rhoton authored a bimonthly article, *Post Conviction Corner*, for Florida Prison Legal Perspectives. Selected articles from *Post Conviction Corner* have been compiled and printed in a legal self-help book, *Postconviction Relief for the Florida Prisoner*. Mr. Rhoton also served on the Board of Directors of the Florida Prisoner's Legal Aid Organization, Inc.

Ryan J. Sydejko, Esq.

Ryan J. Sydejko is an attorney with the law office of Loren Rhoton, P.A. His practice focuses primarily on postconviction matters for those incarcerated throughout the State of Florida. He has argued cases before many circuit courts and District Courts of Appeal and has several published opinions. Mr. Sydejko has also presented cases to the Supreme Court of Florida and the U.S. District Courts for the Middle and Northern Districts of Florida.

Mr. Sydejko graduated from the University of Minnesota with a degree in political science and attended the University of Tulsa College of Law. As a student, he authored a law review article entitled: "International Influence on Democracy: How Terrorism Exploited a Deteriorating Fourth Amendment." The article, exploring how domestic terrorist threats have reshaped everyday law enforcement procedures, was published in the Spring 2006 edition of the Wayne State University Law School Journal of Law in Society. Mr. Sydejko also wrote articles for the Florida Prison Legal Perspectives. Mr. Sydejko is a member in good standing with the Florida Bar and is qualified to practice in all Florida state courts, as well as the Federal District Courts for the Middle and Northern Districts of Florida.

The Florida Postconviction Journal

Volume 1
Issue 2

a quarterly publication of Loren Rhoton, P.A.   **page 3 of 10**

Notable Firm Cases

<u>Dames v. State</u>, 773 So.2d 563 (Fla. 2d DCA 2000) – Improper summary denial of Rule 3.850 Motion reversed & remanded for evidentiary hearing.

<u>Dames v. State</u>, 807 So.2d 756 (Fla. 2d DCA 2002) – First Degree Murder conviction vacated & new trial granted due to ineffective counsel

<u>Battle v. State</u>, 710 So.2d 628 (Fla. 2d DCA 1998) – Improper Habitual Felony Offender Sentence on violation of probation reversed & remanded for resentencing

<u>Mitchell v. State</u>, 734 So.2d 1067 (Fla. 1st DCA 1999) - counsel can render ineffective assistance for failure to argue boarded-up structure is not a 'dwelling' under arson statute

<u>Caban v. State</u>, 9 So.3d 50 (Fla. 5th DCA 2009) – counsel can be ineffective for failing to object to improper impeachment of defense expert witnesses in Shaken Baby Syndrome case

<u>Graff v. State</u>, 846 So.2d 582 (Fla. 2d DCA 2003) – attorney's misadvice as to potential sentence can amount to ineffective assistance of counsel sufficient to justify withdrawal of plea.

<u>Easley v. State</u>, 742 So.2d 463 (Fla. 2d DCA 1999) – counsel can render ineffective assistance for failure to investigate insanity defense.

<u>Campbell v. State</u>, 16 So.3d 316 (Fla. 2d DCA 2009) – Manifest Injustice – summary denial of Rule 3.800 motion to correct illegal sentence reversed & remanded on manifest injustice grounds.

<u>Thompson v. State</u>, 987 So.2d 727 (Fla. 4th DCA 2008) – Reversal of Life Sentences – entitled to *de novo* resentencing upon correction of improper consecutive life sentences for murder and burglary.

<u>Williams v. State</u>, 777 So.2d 947 (Fla. 2000) – Right to Belated Postconviction Motion – if postconviction counsel fails to timely file Rule 3.850 Motion, defendant has right to file belated appeal.

<u>Parker v. State</u>, 977 So.2d 671 (Fla. 4th DCA 2008) – Sentence reversed & remanded for resentencing due to judicial vindictiveness

Improper Bolstering of Co-Defendant's Testimony by Police Warrants Reversal

The Florida Supreme Court recently ruled in a case where a police officer bolstered testimony of a co-defendant in a first-degree murder case. In <u>Tumblin v. State</u>, 29 So.3d 1093 (Fla. 2010), the defendant was charged in the shooting death of a auto shop owner. <u>Id.</u> at 1095. The only eyewitness to the shooting was another suspect, who eventually became a co-defendant. <u>Id.</u> The co-defendant implicated Tumblin as both the mastermind and the gunman. <u>Id.</u> at 1096. In exchange for this information and his testimony at trial, the co-defendant received a plea deal for second-degree murder with a 20-year cap on his sentence. <u>Id.</u>

At trial, a police lieutenant, who took the initial statement from the co-defendant, testified that he believed the co-defendant was telling the truth. <u>Id.</u> at 1101. The Court noted that allowing a witness (the lieutenant) to comment on the credibility of another witness (the co-

defendant) invaded the province of the jury as deciders of credibility. <u>Id.</u> Further aggravating is the fact that testimony from law enforcement is typically afforded greater weight. <u>Id.</u>; *see also* <u>Perez v. State</u>, 595 So.2d 1096, 1097 (Fla. 3d DCA 1992) (stating that improper admission of police officer's testimony to bolster the credibility of a witness cannot be deemed harmless).

Defense counsel did object to the improper statement, and the trial court did strike the comment. <u>Id.</u> at 1101. Even with a curative instruction however, the Court held Tumblin was denied a fair trial as the improperly bolstered testimony of the co-defendant put Tumblin at the scene with a gun in his hand, and pulling the trigger. Because this testimony was instrumental to the jury's finding of first-degree premeditated murder, it's admission denied Tumblin of his right to a fair trial. <u>Id.</u> at 1104.

Support Services for Inmates & Their Families Available

The Florida Postconviction Journal will occasionally recommend groups or services that are beneficial to inmates and their families. If you have an organization that provides advice or assistance to inmates and/or their families, contact us about the possibility of a mention in our newsletter. We have recently discovered R.I.S.E. (Relations of Inmates Supporting Each-Other). R.I.S.E. is an organization that offers support to the friends and families of the Florida incarcerated population. Their programs include a carpool connection, Books for Inmates, a Christmas toy drive for children of inmates, assistance to out-of-state families who are visiting Florida inmates, new visitor seminars, and a newsletter, The Sun-RISE Chronicle. Candy Kendrick is the founder and CEO of R.I.S.E., and she can be reached at <u>RISEFLORIDA@Yahoo.com</u>, or by phone at (941)421-6907. The address for R.I.S.E. is: 23184 Allen Avenue, Port Charlotte, Florida 33980.

Supreme Court Finds Fundamental Error In Use of Standard Jury Instruction

by Ryan J. Sydejko

In State v. Montgomery, 35 Fla. L. Weekly S204 (Fla. 2010), the Florida Supreme Court addressed a significant issue with Florida Standard Jury Instruction (Criminal) 7.7 (2006). In Montgomery, the defendant was charged with first-degree murder, as well as the necessary lesser included offense of second-degree murder and manslaughter. Id. At the time of Montgomery's trial (2007) the instruction read: "To prove the crime of Manslaughter, the State must prove the following two elements beyond a reasonable doubt:

1. (Victim) is dead.
2. (Defendant) intentionally caused the death of (victim).

Id. The problem with such an instruction, according to the Florida Supreme Court, is that a reasonable jury would have to find that the defendant intended to kill the victim, despite the fact that intent to kill is not an element of the offense of manslaughter. See Fla. Stat. § 782.07. Instead, manslaughter requires an intent to commit an act which causes death. In re Standard Jury Instructions in Criminal Cases – Report 2007-10, 997 So.2d 403, 403 (Fla. 2008).

On its face, it would appear beneficial to criminal defendants to force the State to prove this extra element (an intent to kill). But, as in the case of Montgomery, it actually cuts against the defense. Therefore, Montgomery argued that not only was the instruction erroneous, but such an erroneous instruction constituted fundamental error as it deprived him of an accurate manslaughter instruction. As the argument went, the incorrect statement of Florida law deprived Montgomery of the possibility of receiving a conviction for the lesser included offense of manslaughter. For example, the jury did not find Montgomery guilty of first-degree murder, as charged. They jury then, presumably, went down the list of lesser included offenses. It next arrived at second-degree murder, which includes the element of committing a criminal act imminently dangerous to another human being which resulted in death. Note the absence of an intent to kill. Because the jury already decided there was no intent to kill (by foregoing a conviction of first-degree murder), it may have simply arrived at a verdict of guilt of second-degree murder because it was the only offense left that did not include intent to kill. Had the jury been properly instructed, it may have continued down the list of lesser included offenses and found Montgomery guilty of manslaughter instead. In other words, the jury was not permitted the opportunity to consider the appropriate,

permitted the opportunity to consider the appropriate, and necessary, lesser included offense of manslaughter in which the defendant was entitled. State v. Hankerson, 831 So.2d 235, 236-237 (Fla. 1st DCA 2002).

The Court held that criminal defendants are entitled to accurate jury instructions. Reed v. State, 837 So.2d 366, 369 (Fla. 2002). And because manslaughter is a category one lesser included offense of first-degree murder, the jury must be so instructed. See Fla. Std. Jury Instr. (Crim.) 7.2. The erroneous statement of Florida law regarding manslaughter was "pertinent or material to what the jury must consider in order to convict" and therefore constituted fundamental error which can be raised for the first time on appeal.

The question then becomes whether the error was such to warrant vacation of Montgomery's judgment and sentence. The key in Montgomery was that Montgomery was ultimately convicted of the lesser included offense of second-degree murder, an offense only one step removed from manslaughter. The Court has previously held that an erroneous jury instruction of an offense one step removed from the offense for which the defendant was convicted results in per se reversible error. Pena v. State, 901 So.2d 781, 787 (Fla. 2005). When the offense is more than one step removed, the harmless error analysis applies. Id. Because the conviction in Montgomery (second-degree murder) was only one step removed from the erroneously instructed offense (manslaughter), the Court found fundamental error which was per se reversible. Such error can be raised in a timely petition alleging the ineffective assistance of appellate counsel if counsel failed to raise the issue of erroneous manslaughter instructions. Sharpe v. State, 35 Fla. L. Weekly D1154 (Fla. 1st DCA 2010).

Montgomery was rendered on April 8, 2010, and the District Courts of Appeal have moved relatively swiftly in their attempt to limit Montgomery's application. Most notably is the First District Court's decision in Rozzelle v. State, 29 So.3d 1141 (Fla. 1st DCA 2009), which declined to apply Montgomery retroactively to cases that were final prior to Montgomery's issuance. Further, if the defendant is convicted of manslaughter, there is no showing of prejudice. Rivera v. State, 29 So.3d 1139 (Fla. 1st DCA 2009). Therefore, in the event an erroneous manslaughter instruction may have been provided at trial, it is imperative to present a timely claim to the tribunal.

Public Records and Access to the Files of the Office of the State Attorney

by Loren D. Rhoton

When one investigates his or her case for potential postconviction claims he typically reviews pretrial discovery documents, trial transcripts, the record on appeal, and correspondence from the trial attorney. All of these documents are valuable and, when properly reviewed, can present viable postconviction claims. But, an often of overlooked source of potential claims is the State Attorney's file. Said file is, for the most part, a public record and can be viewed by anyone who makes a request. The purpose of this article is to direct interested persons on how to obtain public records such as a prosecutor's file on a criminal case.

Article I, §24(a) of the Florida Constitution provides that: "every person has the right to inspect or copy any public record made or received in connection with the official business of any public body, officer or employee of the state...". In addition to the Florida Constitution, Florida Statutes §119, the *Public Records Act*, is the vehicle which affords the public access to most public information. §119.011 defines public records as "...all documents, papers, letters, maps, books, tapes, photographs, films, sound recordings, data software, or other material, regardless of the physical form, characteristics, or means of transmission, made or received pursuant to law or ordinance or in connection with the transaction of

official business by any agency." In other words, public documents include all materials made or received by an agency in connection with official business that are used to perpetuate, communicate, or formalize knowledge. *See*, Shevin v. Byron, et.al., 379 So. 640 (Fla. 1980). For the most part, any and all records received by a public agency are public records unless they are subject to an exception provided by Chapter 119. For the purposes of this article, important exceptions to be aware of are:

* *Active* criminal investigative and intelligence information

* Attorney "work product" in an active case

* Identity of crime victims

* Addresses and phone numbers of law enforcement officers and former officers and their families

Other exemptions from Chapter 119 can be found in §119.071. But, for the most part, Chapter 119 is based upon the premise that all records of a public agency are public records unless excluded by a specific exemption. The public records law is to be construed liberally in favor of openness, and all

Continued on page 6 ⇒

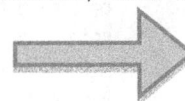

To Subscribe to *The Florida Postconviction Journal*:

The *Florida Postconviction Journal* is currently being provided, free of charge, to Florida inmates who are interested in receiving the helpful advice and information contained in the newsletter. If you wish to have your name added to the newsletter's mailing list, please fill out the form below and mail it to Loren Rhoton, P.A., 412 East Madison Street, Suite 1111, Tampa, FL 33062. For non-inmates interested in subscribing to the newsletter, please forward a money order in the amount of $25 for a one-year subscription.

Name _____ DC# _____

Institution Name and Street Address _____

City _____ State _____ Zip _____

Public Records and Access to the Files of the Office of the State Attorney

(continued from page 5)

exemptions from disclosure are to be construed narrowly and limited to their designated purpose. *See*, City of St. Petersburg v. Romine ex rel. Dillinger, 719 So.2d 19, 23 (Fla. 2nd DCA 1998).

It is important to know that a prosecutor's case file is a public record that can be reviewed by any person who so requests. Of course, State Attorney case files on active cases will be considered to come under the *active criminal investigative* or *criminal intelligence* exemptions of Chapter 119. But, once a criminal case is disposed of and the disposition is final, the entire State Attorney's file on the case becomes a public record under Chapter 119. This means that the entire file (excluding any portions that are covered by a specific exemption) is open to viewing by anybody who makes a public records request.

Of course it is quite possible that the State Attorney's Office may claim that a prosecutor's notes come under the *work product* exception. However, this is frequently not a valid exemption for the State to claim as Florida Statute §119.071(d)(1), provides:

> (d) 1. A public record that was prepared by an agency attorney (including an attorney employed or retained by the agency or employed or retained by another public officer or agency to protect or represent the interests of the agency having custody of the record) or prepared at the attorney's express direction, that reflects a mental impression, conclusion, litigation strategy, or legal theory of the attorney or the agency, and that was prepared exclusively for civil or criminal litigation or for adversarial administrative proceedings, or that was prepared in anticipation of imminent civil or criminal litigation or imminent adversarial administrative proceedings, is exempt from s. 119.07(1) and s. 24(a), Art. I of the State Constitution **until the conclusion of the litigation or adversarial administrative proceedings**. (*Emphasis added*).

In reviewing public records, be sure to be alert for information and or evidence that is noted in the files and was never disclosed to you or your attorney. If any such nuggets should appear, they could potentially provide grounds for a 3.850 motion based upon newly discovered evidence, <u>Brady</u> violations, etc. While it is not possible to list every potential issue that could arise upon the viewing of the prosecutor's files, it is important to note that such a public records request may be very helpful in preparing a postconviction attack on a Judgment and Sentence.

If you are reading this article it is likely that you are incarcerated and will be unable to conduct a review of a prosecutor's files on your own. Therefore, I recommend, if possible, that an attorney experienced in such matters be retained to assist with the request and review of the prosecutor's files. In the alternative, a friend or family member could conduct the search on an incarcerated person's behalf. But, it will be important for the reviewer to be extremely familiar with the facts of the case being reviewed so as to know when something interesting/helpful appears in the prosecutor's file.

Chapter 119 provides that: "Every person who has custody of a public record shall permit the record to be inspected and examined by any person desiring to do so, at any reasonable time, under reasonable conditions, and under supervision by the custodian of the public record or the custodian's designee. The custodian shall furnish a copy or a certified copy of the record upon payment of the fee prescribed by law... and for all other copies, upon payment of the actual cost of duplication of the record." §119.07(1)(a) provides more information on the costs of copies and duplication of records. Be aware that one may incur costs when performing a public records review.

To make a public records request, one must contact the records custodian for the public agency and ask to view specific records. The request does not have to be in writing. *See* §119.07(1)(a). Nevertheless, it is always beneficial to put the request in writing and ask that the custodian specify, in writing, any §119 exemptions it is claiming. It will behoove the public records requestor to make a paper trail in

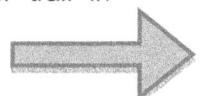

Continued on page 7

Public Records and Access to the Files of the Office of the State Attorney

(continued from page 6)

case he or she needs to bring a civil action to enforce public records viewing rights. Therefore, it is best to make a specific written request for the records one wishes to see. Once the request is made the records custodian must be given a "reasonable time" to retrieve the records and delete any portions that the custodian claims are exempt. Said "reasonable time" is the only delay that is permitted for producing the public records for inspection. The Tribune Company v. Cannella, 458 So.2d 1075 (Fla. 1984).

Once a public records request is made the custodian must permit the inspection at any reasonable time, under reasonable conditions, and under supervision by the custodian of the public record or the custodian's designee. See §119.07(1)(a). The custodian cannot refuse to produce the requested records just because some parts of the record are exempted. Instead, the custodian shall delete or excise the exempted portions and produce the nonexempted record portions. See §119.07)(2)(a). Once again, when making public records requests, it is wise to be aware that the custodian can charge for copies and for extensive use of technology and clerical or supervisory costs. §119.07(1)(b).

If, for some reason, the custodian fails to act on a public records request, the proper remedy is a petition for a writ of mandamus in the appropriate circuit court. Staton v. McMillan, 597 So.2d 940 (Fla.1st DCA 1992). Such a petition should seek to compel the custodian of the records to comply with the public records request. But, before filing a mandamus petition the petitioner must first furnish a public records request to the agency involved. It will help to attach your written public records request as an exhibit to the petition. It is also important to note that if a mandamus petitioner succeeds in obtaining the records via a civil action (mandamus petition) §119.12 provides for attorneys fees. §119.12 specifically provides that "[i]f a civil action is filed against an agency to enforce the provisions of this chapter and if the court determines that such agency unlawfully refused to permit a public record to be inspected, examined, or copied, the court shall assess and award, against the agency responsible, the reasonable costs of enforcement including reasonable attorneys' fees."

A public records search of the prosecutor's file may not always turn up information helpful to a postconviction case. On the other hand, one never knows, the file could be rife with newly discovered evidence claims. Therefore, it is important to consider conducting such a public records search to discover, support or supplement a postconviction claim.

Ineffective Assistance of Counsel and <u>Strickland</u>: Proving the Prejudice Prong

by Ryan J. Sydejko

As many postconviction followers are aware, <u>Strickland v. Washington</u>, 466 U.S. 668 (1984), is one of, if not the most, important cases to understand and apply when pursuing Florida Rule of Criminal Procedure 3.850 motions for postconviction relief. In order to demonstrate that trial counsel rendered ineffective assistance of counsel, a movant must demonstrate: (1) that counsel's conduct was so defective as to fall below an objective standard of reasonableness; and (2) that such conduct prejudiced the movant in that but for counsel's conduct, a different outcome would have probably occurred. <u>Id.</u> at 687. Both prongs must be demonstrated to support postconviction relief. <u>Id.</u> This fact is frequently overlooked by postconviction movants. Remember, even if counsel's conduct was deficient, it must be shown that had counsel performed effectively, a different outcome would probably have occurred.

In <u>Ferrell v. State</u>, 29 So.3d 959 (Fla. 2010), the Florida Supreme Court provided a litany of examples of the failure to demonstrate prejudice. <u>Ferrell</u> is helpful, especially for those proceeding *pro se*, as it illustrates the pitfalls of alleging ineffectiveness without backing it up with much substance. The following were some of the claims addressed by the Supreme Court in <u>Ferrell</u>:

* Ferrell argued that trial counsel was ineffective for failing to depose two witnesses whom testified at trial, as both would have revealed a number of reliability and impeachment issues. <u>Id.</u> at 969. The Court found this allegation conclusory as Ferrell failed to show any "specific evidentiary matter to which the failure to depose witnesses would relate"; failed to state what those issues would be; and failed to allege what evidence would have been discovered. <u>Id.</u> at 969-970. Without any specificity, Ferrell failed to demonstrate prejudice. <u>Id.</u> at 970.

* Ferrell argued that trial counsel was ineffective for failing to attend depositions of two witnesses. <u>Id.</u> Even though the Court acknowledged that counsel's failure to attend depositions was presumed deficient, the Court found that Ferrell failed to establish prejudice as he did not identify any specific information that counsel would have learned by attending the depositions. <u>Id.</u>

* Ferrell next argued that counsel was ineffective due to an inexcused absence from a scheduled hearing date. <u>Id.</u> at 971. The Court found this action deficient, but also found Ferrell failed to demonstrate any prejudice due to counsel's absence from the hearing. <u>Id.</u>

* Ferrell also argued that counsel was ineffective for failing to attend numerous other pretrial hearings. <u>Id.</u> The Court found that counsel either called ahead and informed the Court of his expected absence, or nonsubstantive matters were addressed. <u>Id.</u> Therefore, once again, Ferrell failed to show how he was prejudiced.

* Ferrell argued that counsel was ineffective for conducting an 8-page voir dire while the State took 141-pages. <u>Id.</u> at 973-974. The Court found, again, that Ferrell failed to demonstrate prejudice as he failed to identify any questions counsel should have posed, and failed to identify any juror who, with more extensive questioning, would have been found biased. <u>Id.</u> at 974.

* Ferrell alleged counsel was ineffective for telling the jury during opening statement that an alibi defense would be presented; then, during trial, failing to present said defense. <u>Id.</u> at 975. The Court found no prejudice as counsel sufficiently explained this failure during closing argument. <u>Id.</u>

The Court also went on to address Ferrell's <u>Giglio</u> and <u>Brady</u> claims, among many others, which failed to rise to the level of reversible error. The issue that finally garnered Ferrell relief pertained to his purportedly unknowing and involuntary waiver of evidence during the penalty phase of his capital murder trial. <u>Id.</u> at 983. Ferrell was subsequently awarded a new penalty phase proceeding.

The most important aspect of this case, for non-capital felony defendants, is the importance of alleging and clearly demonstrating prejudice. Many litigants focus primarily on counsel's conduct, and its impropriety, and conclude their motions with brief, conclusory statements that they were prejudiced. In order to satisfy <u>Strickland</u>, it is important to not only identify exactly how the conduct was prejudicial, but also how it would have affected the outcome without the ineffectiveness. Reviewing Ferrell's arguments can provide a great tutorial in avoiding blanket arguments and actually getting specific with one's claims.

Overview of Procedure for Restoring Forfeited Gain Time

Submitted by Guest Columnist Melvin Perez

This article will provide an overview to the procedure required for restoring gain time forfeited due to disciplinary reports (DR's) or violations of any form of supervised release.

Under the rule, gain time that has been forfeited under the current commitment due to disciplinary action or revocation of parole, probation, community control, provisional release, supervised community control, conditional medical release, control release or conditional release shall be subject to restoration when the restoration would produce the same or greater benefits as those derived from the forfeiture in the first place. Fla. Admin. Code 33-601.105(1).

However, only those prisoners whose adjustment and performance since the forfeiture comply with, and exceed, all behavioral objectives are eligible for consideration. Moreover, the restoration shall only be considered when the prisoner has clearly performed positively over a period of tiem and it appears the prisoner will continue this positive adjustment without further violations of Department of Corrections rules or the law of the State of Florida. The rule also provides that the prisoner must be serving that portion of the sentence which, but for the forfeiture of gain time, would have been completed. Further, there must be an elapsed time of at least one-year since the last disciplinary action occurred if the forfeiture resulted from a DR. Fla. Admin. Code 33-601.105(2)(a). Equally important, the prisoner must have completed or be participating in all available programs recommended by the classification team.

In contrast, a prisoner is ineligible if he or she has been convicted of a felony during the current commitment or if found guilty of any of a number of rule violations. See Fla. Admin. Code § 33-601.105(2)(a)(4). Once the prisoner has gain time restored, subsequent loss of gain time due to DR's makes the prisoner ineligible for further restoration. Gain time lost before a prisoner is convicted of an additional felony while incarcerated will not be considered for restoration.

If the forfeiture results from a violation of any type of the aforementioned release supervisions, there must also be a one-year lapse and the prisoner will only be considered if he was not convicted for a new offense that occurred during the release period. Likewise, the prisoner must be DR free since return of the violation, and have completed or be participating in all available recommended programs. Any prisoner who receives the restoration due to a violation will not be eligible for such on any subsequent violations.

A prisoner will only be considered for restoration if he or she meets the requirements in subsections (1) and (2). But, there is no entitlement for consideration. The prisoner must submit a request to his classification officer who must determine if the prisoner meets the criteria. If the prisoner meets such criteria, the request shall be forwarded to the Institutional Classification Team (ICT) with a recommendation either for or against restoration. In turn, if the prisoner does not meet the criteria, the classification officer shall return the request to the prisoner indicating in writing which criteria have not been met.

The ICT shall consider the request based upon the criteria described in subsections (1) and (2). If the ICT recommends restoration, the recommendation shall be forwarded to the Assistant Secretary of Institutions or designee for final action. On the other hand, if the ICT does not make a recommendation for restoration, the request shall be returned to the prisoner along with the basis for the denial. If the ICT's basis for the denial fails to comply with the rules or are unreasonable, the prisoner may file a formal grievance challenging the ICT's basis. The ICT's failure to follow the rule in denying the request can be challenged through a mandamus action after exhausting administrative remedies. While the act of granting the restoration is discretionary, DOC must comply with the rules. Although a writ of mandamus cannot be used to compel a public agency to exercise its discretionary power in a given manner, it may be used to compel the agency to follow its own rules. Rivera v. Moore, 825 So.2d 505 (Fla. 1st DCA 2005).

Upon receipt of the recommendation from the ICT, the final approving authority shall approve or deny the recommendation based upon the applicable criteria. The institution will be notified and the facility staff must notify the prisoner of the decision and the basis for the decision.

Loren Rhoton, P.A.

Postconviction Attorneys

412 East Madison Street
Suite 1111
Tampa, Florida 33602
Tel: 813-226-3138
Fax: 813-221-2182
Email:
lorenrhoton@rhotonpostconviction.com
rsydejko@rhotonpostconviction.com

- Direct Appeals
- Belated Appeals
- Rule 3.850 Motions
- Illegal Sentence Corrections
- Rule 9.141 Petitions
- Federal Habeas Corpus Petitions
- Clemency Petitions and Waivers

The Florida Postconviction Journal publishes up to four times per year. You are receiving this due to your previous subscription or interest with Florida Prison Legal Perspectives. This Journal provides resources for information affecting prisoners, their families, friends, loved ones, and the general public of the State of Florida. Promoting skilled access to the court system for indigent prisoners is a primary goal of this publication. Due to the volume of mail that is received, not all correspondence can be returned. If you would like return of materials, please enclose a postage-paid and pre-addressed envelope. This publication is not meant to be a substitute for legal or other professional advice. The material addressed in the Journal should not be relied upon as authoritative and may not contain sufficient information to deal with specific legal issues.

The Florida Postconviction Journal
a publication of Loren Rhoton, P.A.
412 East Madison Street
Suite 1111
Tampa, FL 33602

CHANGE SERVICE REQUESTED

Name
Institution
Street Address
City, State, Zip

The Florida Postconviction Journal

Volume 1
Issue 3

a quarterly publication of Loren Rhoton, P.A.

Winter 2010

Lame Ducks, Dead Hippies & New Year's Wishes

by Loren D. Rhoton

Okay, so, the good news is that if you are a long-dead rock star with a misdemeanor conviction, you'll have no problem getting clemency relief in Florida. On the other hand, if you are an actual living human being who has legitimate grounds to request clemency, you will have to wait at least two years before the Florida Clemency Board will even consider whether or not to allow you to petition for executive clemency. That's right, the Florida Clemency Board and Charley Crist recently granted a pardon to Jim Morrison, singer for 60's psychedelic rock band, The Doors. Charley Crist said that he did so because, after reviewing the evidence, he believed that Morrison might not be guilty. I'm sure this is pretty interesting to the hoards of inmates who have been explicitly told by the Clemency Board that the board does not retry cases.

Anyway, aside from my wanting to vent about how ludicrous it is for the Clemency Board to grant a pardon to a dead anti-hero (albeit a very cool one) who would have wiped his @#$ with the pardon if he were alive, I guess the point is this: We are coming into a new year with a new Governor and hopefully some big changes will be made with regard to the clemency process. Whether that is realistic or not, I do not know.

Regardless, my wish for all of my readers this year is that you can get the post conviction and/or clemency relief that each and every one of you deserves. So along with my newsletter, I send out my best wishes for a happy and productive new year. In keeping with my wish, I once again hope that you find the advice in this newsletter to be helpful and informative about how to attack your judgment and sentences. I hope that you empower yourselves with this information and use it to your benefit. And hey, let's hope that incoming Governor Rick Scott doesn't allow the Clemency Board to get mired down in clemency petitions from teen heartthrob David Cassidy or funk superstar George Clinton.

Prosecutor's "No Other Reasonable Explanation But Guilt" Closing Argument Improper

In Evans v. State, 26 So.3d 85 (Fla. 2d DCA 2010), the Court was again presented with an allegation of improper prosecutorial comments during closing argument. A brief recitation of the facts is necessary: in 2005 the Pinellas County Sheriff's Office executed a search warrant on a suspected drug house. Id. at 87-88. Upon entering, eight individuals were found inside. Id. at 88. The defendant was found in the bathroom, on the toilet, directly across the hall from the bedroom. Id. At that time, the defendant was wearing rubber gloves and possessed nearly $1,800 in twenty dollar bills. Id. In the bedroom across the hall, officers found more rubber gloves, crack cocaine, razors, a drug ledger, rental car keys and a digital scale. Id. Officers believed that bedroom was used as the production and distribution center for the crack cocaine, and opined that the defendant's rubber gloves were used to protect himself during that process. Id. The defendant was tried and convicted of drug trafficking. Id. at 87.

Because the cocaine was found in a separate room from the defendant in a house with numerous occupants, the State had to prove Evans had constructive possession of the drugs. Id. at 89.

To do so, the prosecutor argued during closing that "if [Evans] wasn't guilty, wouldn't there be some reasonable explanation for him wearing those gloves." Id. at 91. He continued: "And be very clear, evidence that there is no reasonable explanation for him having those gloves on except that he was in control of the east bedroom." Id. Counsel's repeated objections and motion for mistrial were overruled. Id. The Second DCA ultimately held that the prosecutor's statements amounted to improper comment on the defendant's right not to testify. Id. at 91-92. Such argument could effectively cause the jury to believe that the defendant was required to introduce evidence or testify in his own defense. As a result, a new trial was granted. Id. at 92.

About Loren Rhoton, P.A.

Loren Rhoton, P.A. is a law firm that focuses exclusively on postconviction actions and inmate issues. The mission of Loren Rhoton, P.A. is to ensure that justice is accomplished in each and every case the firm undertakes. The firm's area of practice ranges from direct criminal appeals and postconviction actions to assisting inmates in dealing with the Florida Department of Corrections. Loren Rhoton, P.A., is a small firm, consisting of Mr. Loren D. Rhoton and Mr. Ryan J. Sydejko. The firm strives to keep a small caseload in order to give each case the individual attention it deserves. We are not a volume business. We do not accept every case that is presented to the firm for representation. A thorough review of any potential case will be conducted before the firm undertakes full representation. If you wish to have your case reviewed for representation, please contact Loren Rhoton for more information. If inquiring about representation, please do not send any materials to the firm that you wish to have returned to you.

Loren D. Rhoton, Esq.

Loren D. Rhoton is an attorney in private practice with the law office of Loren Rhoton, P.A., in Tampa, Florida. Mr. Rhoton graduated from the University of Toledo College of Law and has been a member in good standing with The Florida Bar since his admission to practice in 1995. The exclusive focus of Mr. Rhoton's practice is dedicated to assisting Florida inmates with their criminal appeal/postconviction cases.

Mr. Rhoton is a member of The Florida Bar's Appellate Division. He is also a member of the U.S. District Court, in and for the Middle and Northern Districts of Florida. Mr. Rhoton is licensed to practice before the U.S. Court of Appeals for the 11th Circuit and is also certified to practice before the U.S. Supreme Court. Mr. Rhoton regularly practices before Federal District Courts and the U.S. Court of Appeals for the 11th Circuit.

Mr. Rhoton typically deals with clients who have lengthy prison sentences. Mr. Rhoton has investigated and pursued hundreds of postconviction cases. He has practiced in all phases of the Florida Judicial System, all the way from misdemeanor county courts up to the Florida Supreme Court. Additionally, Mr. Rhoton has been directly responsible for amendments to Florida Rule of Criminal Procedure 3.850 (the main vehicle for most postconviction actions). Mr. Rhoton is appointed by the Florida Supreme Court to the Florida Criminal Rules Steering Committee, Subcommittee on Postconviction Relief, which is focused on rewriting Florida Rule of Criminal Procedure 3.850. Mr. Rhoton works on said subcommittee with judges and other governmental officials in an effort to improve the administration and execution of postconviction proceedings. Mr. Rhoton's role on said committee has been to advocate for changes that will be beneficial to postconviction litigants (inmates).

For over a decade, Mr. Rhoton authored a bimonthly article, *Post Conviction Corner*, for Florida Prison Legal Perspectives. Selected articles from *Post Conviction Corner* have been compiled and printed in a legal self-help book, *Postconviction Relief for the Florida Prisoner*. Mr. Rhoton also served on the Board of Directors of the Florida Prisoner's Legal Aid Organization, Inc.

Ryan J. Sydejko, Esq.

Ryan J. Sydejko is an attorney with the law office of Loren Rhoton, P.A. His practice focuses primarily on postconviction matters for those incarcerated throughout the State of Florida. He has argued cases before many circuit courts and District Courts of Appeal and has several published opinions. Mr. Sydejko has also presented cases to the Supreme Court of Florida and the U.S. District Courts for the Middle and Northern Districts of Florida.

Mr. Sydejko graduated from the University of Minnesota with a degree in political science and attended the University of Tulsa College of Law. As a student, he authored a law review article entitled: "International Influence on Democracy: How Terrorism Exploited a Deteriorating Fourth Amendment." The article, exploring how domestic terrorist threats have reshaped everyday law enforcement procedures, was published in the Spring 2006 edition of the Wayne State University Law School Journal of Law in Society. Mr. Sydejko also wrote articles for the Florida Prison Legal Perspectives. Mr. Sydejko is a member in good standing with the Florida Bar and is qualified to practice in all Florida state courts, as well as the Federal District Courts for the Middle and Northern Districts of Florida.

The Florida Postconviction Journal

Volume 1
Issue 3

a quarterly publication of Loren Rhoton, P.A.

page 3 of 10

Notable Firm Cases

<u>Dames v. State</u>, 773 So.2d 563 (Fla. 2d DCA 2000) – Improper summary denial of Rule 3.850 Motion reversed & remanded for evidentiary hearing.

<u>Dames v. State</u>, 807 So.2d 756 (Fla. 2d DCA 2002) – First Degree Murder conviction vacated & new trial granted due to ineffective counsel

<u>Battle v. State</u>, 710 So.2d 628 (Fla. 2d DCA 1998) – Improper Habitual Felony Offender Sentence on violation of probation reversed & remanded for resentencing

<u>Mitchell v. State</u>, 734 So.2d 1067 (Fla. 1st DCA 1999) - counsel can render ineffective assistance for failure to argue boarded-up structure is not a 'dwelling' under arson statute

<u>Caban v. State</u>, 9 So.3d 50 (Fla. 5th DCA 2009) – counsel can be ineffective for failing to object to improper impeachment of defense expert witnesses in Shaken Baby Syndrome case

<u>Graff v. State</u>, 846 So.2d 582 (Fla. 2d DCA 2003) – attorney's misadvice as to potential sentence can amount to ineffective assistance of counsel sufficient to justify withdrawal of plea.

<u>Easley v. State</u>, 742 So.2d 463 (Fla. 2d DCA 1999) – counsel can render ineffective assistance for failure to investigate insanity defense.

<u>Campbell v. State</u>, 16 So.3d 316 (Fla. 2d DCA 2009) – Manifest Injustice – summary denial of Rule 3.800 motion to correct illegal sentence reversed & remanded on manifest injustice grounds.

<u>Thompson v. State</u>, 987 So.2d 727 (Fla. 4th DCA 2008) – Reversal of Life Sentences – entitled to *de novo* resentencing upon correction of improper consecutive life sentences for murder and burglary.

<u>Williams v. State</u>, 777 So.2d 947 (Fla. 2000) – Right to Belated Postconviction Motion – if post-conviction counsel fails to timely file Rule 3.850 Motion, defendant has right to file belated appeal.

<u>Parker v. State</u>, 977 So.2d 671 (Fla. 4th DCA 2008) – Sentence reversed & remanded for resentencing due to judicial vindictiveness

Officer's Opinion that Defendant Acted Like Typical Drug Trafficker is Error

In Austin v. State, 44 So.3d 1260 (Fla. 1st DCA 2010), the First District Court of Appeal found reversible error when a Florida State Trooper testified at trial that the defendant acted like a typical drug trafficker. Id. at 1261-1262. The trooper, who was neither tendered nor accepted as an expert witness, testified that drug traffickers frequently utilize third-party rental cars so they can disclaim any drugs which may be found in the vehicle; or, so the suspect can flee from the vehicle and not be traced back to it. Id. at 1262. Defense counsel objected, but the trial court permitted the testimony, holding that "these are factors [law enforcement] are taught to look for, which makes it a relevant area of inquiry." Id. The error was compounded by the prosecutor when he reiterated the trooper's testimony during closing, arguing that it was sound drug trafficking practice to use third-party rental cars so as to avoid law enforcement detection. Id.

The First DCA began by noting: "testimony about the general behavior of certain kinds of offenders is inadmissible as substantive proof of a defendant's guilt." Id. Such characteristics may give rise to suspicion, but is inadmissible to prove a drug offense was committed. Id. The Court further noted the danger of allowing officers to testify as the trooper did, as it invites juries to convict the defendant by association, rather than on the evidence presented at trial. Id.

The trooper's testimony was not harmless error because it directly negated the defense. Id. at 1263. The defendant asserted that his wife had rented the vehicle and, unbeknownst to the defendant, the vehicle contained large quantities of drugs. Id. The State offered no evidence that the defendant actually knew of the drugs. Id. Essentially, the trooper's testimony allowed the State to avoid proving the element of knowledge by instructing the jury to assume the defendant knew of the drugs because he was acting like a drug trafficker. Id. For these reasons, the Court found the trooper's testimony regarding general behavior patterns of drug traffickers to be reversible error.

Pro Se Postconviction Appellate Briefing: Which Issues to Include in the Initial Brief?

by Ryan J. Sydejko

A trial court may utilize any number of rationales for denying postconviction claims. Some commonly utilized rationales include: untimeliness (Fla. R. Crim. P. 3.850(b)), successiveness (Fla. R. Crim. P. 3.850(f)), facial insufficiency (Spera v. State, 971 So.2d 754 (Fla. 2007)), and simple denial on the merits. While the trial court has many rationales available, all denials fall into two procedural categories: summary or post-evidentiary hearing. A postconviction movant must be cognizant of the procedural mechanism used by the trial court when preparing the initial brief to the District Court of Appeal. This article focuses on the varying briefing procedures as dictated by the trial court's denial.

Appeals from the denial of postconviction relief are governed by Florida Rule of Appellate Procedure 9.141. If the trial court did not conduct an evidentiary hearing in the case, the appellant is permitted, but not required, to file an initial brief. Fla. R. Crim. P. 9.141(b)(2)(C). If the appellant chooses to so file, the brief is due within fifteen days of the filing of the notice of appeal. Id.

In the event the trial court did conduct an evidentiary hearing on the claims, then the appellant is required to file an initial brief on appeal. Fla. R. Crim. P. 9.141 (b)(3)(C).

Such a procedure appears relatively straightforward: if the trial court granted an evidentiary hearing on the claims, and appeal is taken, then an appellate brief on the issues is required. Fla. R. Crim. P. 9.141(b)(2)(C). If the trial court summarily denied the issues, then an appellant can opt not to file a brief and rely on previous pleadings in support of his/her position. See Fla. R. Crim. P. 9.141(b)(2)(C). A dilemma arises, however, regarding multi-issue postconviction motions, when an evidentiary hearing is held as to some claims, while other claims are summarily denied.

It is fairly common for postconviction movants to raise multiple grounds for relief in Rule 3.850 motions. In fact, such a practice is important as, in most cases, only a single Rule 3.850 motion will be permitted. Fla. R. Crim. P. 3.850(f) ("A second . . . motion may be dismissed if the judge finds that it fails to allege new or different grounds . . . or, if new and different grounds are alleged, the judge finds that the failure of the movant or the attorney to assert those grounds in a prior motion constituted an abuse of the procedure."). Thus, appellants, especially those proceeding pro se, are placed in a difficult position: utilize limited page space to brief arguably improperly summarily denied claims; or,

focus on the claims that had an evidentiary hearing, and allow the appellate court to review the summarily denied claims on its own. The appellate courts are split on how to proceed under such circumstances.

In Walton v. State, 35 Fla. L. Weekly D856 (Fla. 2d DCA 2010), the Second District Court of Appeal addressed a situation in which a postconviction movant had filed a Rule 3.850 motion alleging twenty-four grounds for relief. Id. at *1. All claims were eventually denied by the trial court, but in different manners: some were denied as clearly refuted by the record; some were procedurally barred; some were facially insufficient or conclusory; and two were denied on the merits after an evidentiary hearing. Id. On appeal, Walton focused his briefing on those issues denied as procedurally barred and those clearly refuted by the record. Id.

The appellate court affirmed those grounds which the trial court found clearly refuted by the record, as well as those grounds found to be procedurally barred. Id. The appellate court did, however, reverse the trial court's holding on the eight grounds previously deemed facially insufficient. Id. The appellate court acted despite the fact that these grounds were not briefed by Walton. The appellate court reasoned that it had the inherent power to reverse and remand improperly summarily denied grounds despite a lack of briefing, pursuant to Fla. R. App. P. 9.141(b)(2)(D) which deals with summarily denied postconviction issues. Id. Subsection (D) states: "Unless the record shows conclusively that the appellant is entitled to no relief, the order shall be reversed and the cause remanded for an evidentiary hearing or other appropriate relief." Fla. R. Crim. P. 9.141(b)(2)(D).

The Second DCA interpreted that provision to mean that the appellate court is required to review all summarily denied claims. Id.

In dissent, Judge Kelly argued that when an appellant chooses not to brief a particular issue, the appellant implicitly abandons that issue. Id. at 3. Judge Kelly relied on the position that the appellate court lacks critical information when ruling on un-briefed issues, as the appellant does not state his

Continued on next page

belief why the trial court's ruling was incorrect, the State/Appellee is not afforded a reasonable opportunity to state their position on the un-briefed issue, and the appellate court is not even instructed whether the appellant desires to pursue the ground. Id. Without this information, Judge Kelly "see[s] no reason why we should not conclude that [Walton] has abandoned those claims." Id. at 4.

More recently, the Fourth DCA has echoed Judge Kelly's position. See Prince v. State, 40 So.3d 11 (Fla. 4th DCA 2010). In Prince, the Court held that any non-briefed grounds are waived by the appellant. Id. at 12. In a nod to Walton, the Fourth DCA conceded that briefs are not required in appeals from summary denial of Rule 3.850 motions. Id. at 13. But, the court wrote, should an appellant opt to file a brief, the brief must present argument as to all grounds the appellant feels contain error. Id. Justifying this position, the court noted that appellate courts "may be needlessly reviewing many claims which the appellant no longer disputes." Id.

Not only did the Prince court certify conflict with Walton, but the court also made a specific request: to amend the Florida Rules of Appellate Procedure to permit the district courts to require postconviction appellants to file initial briefs in all cases. Prince, 40 So.3d at 13. This request arguably implies that the Fourth DCA recognizes that the Rules, as currently drafted, do not entirely support their position. The Prince court certified conflict with the Walton decision and has not yet been resolved by the Florida Supreme Court.

The moral of this story is quite simple: in the case of mixed summary and non-summary post-conviction denials, as a pro se appellant, brief all issues believed to have been ruled in error by the trial court. This may very well be a burdensome task for the untrained pro se appellant. Of course, the Florida Supreme Court may eventually resolve this conflict in favor of the Second DCA's position in Walton; but, until then, it is vital for pro se postconviction movants to fully brief each and every issue in order to avoid Price-like involuntary waivers.

Support Services for Inmates & Their Families Available

If you have a suggestion for a group or inmate resource that should be listed in our newsletter, please contact us with the information and we will share any helpful information in future issues.

Innocence Project of Florida.
1100 East Park Ave.
Tallahassee, FL, 32301
Phone: (850) 561-6767
   Assists inmates with postconviction DNA innocence cases and helps exonerees in obtaining compensation for wrongful convictions.

R.I.S.E. (Relations of Inmates Supporting Each-Other).
23184 Allen Avenue,
Port Charlotte, FL, 33980
Phone: (941)421-6907
Contact: Candy Kendrick
Email: RISEFLORIDA@Yahoo.com
   Offers support to the friends and families of Florida inmates. Programs include a carpool connection, Books for Inmates, a Christmas toy drive for children of inmates, assistance to out-of-state families visiting Florida inmates, new visitor seminars, and a newsletter.

Florida Legal Services. www.floridalegalhelp.org
2121 Delta Blvd., Tallahassee, FL, 32303
Phone: (904) 385-7900
   Provides referrals in civil matters.

Prisontalk.com.   An Internet community/forum that provides general information and networking for families of inmates. Also, has Florida specific forum that addresses issues ranging from dealing with the D.O.C. to coping with incarceration.

Florida Justice Institute, Inc.
4320 Bank of America Tower
100 S.E. Second Street
Miami, FL, 33131
Phone: (305) 358-2081
Contact: Randall C. Berg, Jr.
Email: rcberg@floridajusticeinstitute.org
   Handles civil-rights cases regarding conditions in prisons and jails; advocates and lobbies on behalf of prisoners.

To Subscribe or Change Your Mailing Address to *The Florida Postconviction Journal:*

The *Florida Postconviction Journal* is currently being provided, free of charge, to Florida inmates who are interested in receiving the helpful advice and information contained in the newsletter. If you wish to have your name added to the newsletter's mailing list, please fill out the form below and mail it to Loren Rhoton, P.A., 412 East Madison Street, Suite 1111, Tampa, FL 33062. For non-inmates interested in subscribing to the newsletter, please forward a money order in the amount of $25 for a one-year subscription.

Please Check One:

☐ New Subscriber

☐ Change of Address

Name _____ DC# _____

Institution Name and Street Address _____

City _____ State _____ Zip _____

Did the Offense Really Occur in a Dwelling?

by Loren D. Rhoton

The question of whether a building or property is a "dwelling" can become a very relevant issue when determining the level of certain offenses. For example, a simple burglary (one where there is no assault or battery and the defendant is not armed) of a *dwelling* amounts to a second degree punishable by 15 years imprisonment. F.S. §810.02(3). On the other hand, if the act committed was actually simple burglary of an unoccupied structure or conveyance (as opposed to a dwelling), the offense is a 3rd degree felony, punishable by up to 5 years incarceration. F.S. §810.02(4). Likewise, the nature of a building as a dwelling or structure is relevant to the charge of arson. Arson of a dwelling is a 1st degree felony, punishable by up to 30 years. F.S., §806.01(1)(a). But, arson of an unoccupied structure is a 2nd degree felony. F.S., §806.01(2). Thus, the question of whether a building is a *dwelling* or a *structure* can make a great deal of difference in the ultimate sentence in a burglary or arson case. This is an element of burglary and arson cases that is sometimes overlooked and is worth investigating for any defendants convicted of burglary or arson of a dwelling.

F.S. §810.011(2) provides that "dwelling" means "a building or conveyance of any kind, including any attached porch, whether such building or conveyance is temporary or permanent, mobile or immobile, which has a roof over it and is designed to be occupied by people lodging therein at night, together with the curtilage thereof."

Thus, there are many factors that must be analyzed to determine whether a building or property is a dwelling. One such question is whether the property at issue is a part of the curtilage (the land or yard adjoining a house). A common question is if an unattached garage is part of the curtilage of a dwelling. In Martinez v. State, 700 So.2d 142 (Fla. 5th DCA 1997), it was held that an unattached garage from which the defendant stole a tool was not part of the curtilage of the home. In Martinez the defendant was convicted of burglary of a dwelling. The burglary of a dwelling conviction arose from Martinez's theft of a tool from the garage of the victim's home. The victim testified that a driveway ran from the street to his two-car garage. The victim further said that the garage was not attached to his home and that his property was not enclosed with a fence. Martinez argued at trial that the garage was not part of the curtilage and, thus, he could not be found guilty of burglary of a dwelling. The trial court disagreed and Martinez was found guilty of burglary of a dwelling.

On appeal, the Fifth DCA noted that the Florida Supreme Court addressed the issue of what constitutes "curtilage" for the purposes of the burglary statute in

Continued on next page ⇨

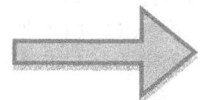

<u>State v. Hamilton</u>, 660 So.2d 1038 (Fla. 1996). The <u>Hamilton</u> Court held that "some form of an enclosure [is necessary] in order for the area surrounding a residence to be considered part of the 'curtilage' as referred to in the burglary statute." The <u>Martinez</u> Court then noted that to enclose commonly means to surround on all sides. <u>Martinez</u> at 143. As such, it was held that the property in question was not "enclosed." Consequently, Martinez's conviction for burglary of a dwelling was vacated and the case was remanded for the trial court to enter a judgment of guilty of the lesser-included charge of burglary of a structure. <u>Id.</u> at 144.

Another relevant question regarding a building's dwelling status is whether the building is habitable. For the purpose of establishing that a 1st degree arson of a dwelling has been committed, the temporary absence of tenants will not cause the house to lose its character as a dwelling if the absence is not unreasonably prolonged and there is an intention to return. But, a house which is abandoned as a dwelling and closed up, or which is converted to some purpose other than human occupancy, ceases to be a dwelling. <u>Sawyer v. State</u>, 132 So. 188 (Fla. 1931); <u>PPM v. State</u>, 447 So. 2d 445 (Fla. 2nd DCA 1984); and <u>Mitchell v. State</u>, 734 So.2d 1067 (1st DCA 1999). In <u>Mitchell</u>, the 1st DCA noted that the "dwelling" in question had been vacant from 1994 through 1996 and had been cited with numerous housing violations that made the building uninhabitable. As such, the <u>Mitchell</u> Court held that a "vacant, damaged, boarded-up house is not a 'dwelling' within the meaning of section 806.01…when there is no evidence the owners intend to return." <u>Mitchell</u> at 1068.

In light of the above, it is always worthwhile to investigate whether a building is actually a dwelling for the purposes of a burglary or arson conviction. These questions are often overlooked by trial attorneys and can result in a defendant being convicted of a more serious offense than the offense that actually occurred. The question of a building's status as a dwelling can be raised on appeal if properly preserved at trial. Or, alternatively, if trial counsel failed to address the issue, it can be raised in a Rule 3.850 motion as a claim of ineffectiveness of counsel for failure to challenge the dwelling status of the building in question. (That is what happened in <u>Mitchell</u>). If said issue is raised in a 3.850 motion, both ineffectiveness of counsel and resulting prejudice must be demonstrated, as per the ineffectiveness test enunciated in <u>Strickland v. Washington</u>, 466 U.S. 668 (1984). Either way, it is always worth considering if the property in question actually qualifies as a dwelling for the purpose of the burglary and arson statutes because reduction in the severity of the offense will likely result in a significant reduction of the resulting sentence.

Defendant Entitled to Resentencing Twenty-One Years After Sentencing Guidelines Declared Unconstitutional

In Williams v. State, 35 Fla. L. Weekly D2396, the Third District Court of Appeal reversed and remanded for resentencing a case in which a defendant was sentenced under a scheme later held unconstitutional. The procedural history of the case is critical.

In 1967, the defendant (Williams) was convicted and sentenced to life for first-degree murder. Id. at *1. The defendant was ultimately paroled. Id.

On October 1, 1983, new sentencing guidelines went into effect. Fla. Stat. § 921.001(4)(1) (1983). On October 13, 1983, the defendant committed, and was later convicted of, aggravated assault and sale of cocaine. Williams at *1. Williams was sentenced to four years incarceration with a three year minimum mandatory sentence, pursuant to the 1983 guidelines. Id. The four year sentence was imposed consecutively to the life sentence. Id.

In 1989, the Florida Supreme Court found the 1983 sentencing guidelines unconstitutional for the period of October 1, 1983 through June 30, 1984. Id. Thus, any persons whose crimes date was between those dates "were entitled to be resentenced." Id.; see also Smith v. State, 537 So.2d 982, 987 (Fla. 1989).

The State of Florida countered, arguing that Williams' postconviction endeavor should have been procedurally denied, as Williams previously raised a similar claim. Williams at *1. The District Court rejected this argument, finding the manifest injustice exception applicable as Williams received a lengthier sentence than would otherwise have been permissible. Id.; see also State v. McBride, 848 So.2d 287, 291-292 (Fla. 2003).

The State alternatively argued that in 1984, when Williams was sentenced, Williams had made an affirmative election to be sentenced under the 1983 sentencing scheme. Williams at *2. The District Court found this argument entirely unpersuasive since, at the time of sentencing, sentencing under the 1983 guidelines was mandatory. Id. Therefore, Williams could not possibly have made any such election. Id.

As of 2010, Williams had yet to receive the resentencing to which he was "entitled." Williams at *1. Thus, the District Court reversed and remanded, directing the trial court to appoint an attorney and hold a resentencing hearing. Id. at *2.

Appellate Counsel Ineffective for Failing to Seek Supplementation of Argument

In Asberry v. State, 32 So.3d 718 (Fla. 1st DCA 2010), the First District Court of Appeal addressed appellate counsel's failure to request permission to supplement argument during a direct appeal.

Asberry, the defendant, was convicted of murder in Duval County, Florida. Id. at 719. He appealed to the First DCA and appellate counsel filed an initial brief on July 30, 2008. Id. The State then responded, filing an answer brief in October 2008. Id. Without any further filings, the First DCA issued its ruling on March 26, 2009. Id. Appellate counsel's ineffectiveness arose, however, from his (or her) failure to seek supplemental argument based upon a similar case ruled on by the First DCA in the interim. Id. In that case, the court found fundamental error based upon defective jury instructions. Id. (citing Montgomery v. State, 34 Fla. L. Weekly D360 (Fla. 1st DCA, February 12, 2009). Asberry subsequently petitioned the First

DCA, alleging that appellate counsel was ineffective for failing to bring the Montgomery decision to the attention of the court. Because the same erroneous jury instruction was given in both Asberry and Montgomery, the court was compelled to find Asberry's appellate counsel ineffective.

It is important to remember that criminal law is an ever evolving body. Especially in today's environment, where cases may remain pending for months or years, a petitioner and his counsel must remain vigilant in researching and updating any applicable case law. Of course, this may also work to a petitioner's detriment should case law arise which counters the petitioner's claims. Ethics require counsel to also present this new case law. Doing so builds a vital rapport and lends credibility to both the petitioner and his counsel. As the pro se litigant likely already knows, never stop researching!

The Florida Postconviction Journal

Volume 1
Issue 3

a quarterly publication of Loren Rhoton, P.A.

Inadequate Plea Colloquy Allows Former Juvenile Offender to Withdraw Plea Five Years Later

by Ryan J. Sydejko

The Fourth District Court of Appeal was recently presented with the following situation in State v. S.S., 40 So.3d 6 (4th DCA 2010): In March 2003, a juvenile, S.S. entered a no contest plea (the offense is not identified in the court's opinion). Id. at 7. Adjudication was withheld and the juvenile was placed on probation, which was ultimately successfully completed in November 2003. Id.

In December 2007, the juvenile applied for a position in a nursing program and learned that her criminal record could not be sealed or expunged. Id. As a result, in June 2008, the juvenile filed a Rule 3.850 Motion for Postconviction Relief alleging her plea was involuntary. Id. As expected, the State immediately responded that the juvenile's motion was untimely. Id.

The juvenile then filed a "Petition for Writ of Error Coram Nobis" alleging that: (1) the plea had not knowingly been entered; and (2) counsel affirmatively misadvised the juvenile regarding her eligibility for expunction of her criminal record. Id. at 7 n.1. (Sidenote: coram nobis is an infrequently used common law vehicle for asserting that the court's previous ruling was premised on alleged errors of fact). Basically, the juvenile argued that she was unaware of the consequences of her plea. Id. at 7. The requested relief was withdrawal of the plea. Id. The State again adopted their typical rationale for denial, asserting that the juvenile's petition was fatally flawed because: (1) the petition was untimely; (2) the petition was legally insufficient; and (3) the juvenile had failed to demonstrate prejudice. Id.

The trial court held an evidentiary hearing and made several critical findings. Id. First, the trial court found the plea colloquy into the juvenile's comprehension of the plea offer absent, thereby constituting fundamental error. Id. Secondly, it was found that counsel provided affirmative misadvice regarding expunction of the criminal record. Id. The sum of these errors led the court to find "the plea colloquy was insufficient to the point of being void." Id. Because the petition was timely (filed within 1-year of discovery that the criminal record could not be sealed), the court held:

"Now based upon that, and I say this with some reluctance, the Court finds that with those findings, the Court has the obligation to grant the motion."

Id. at 8. The State appealed. Id.

The Fourth DCA begins analysis by noting that the State possessed no statutory authority for taking appeal from an order permitting a defendant to withdraw a plea. Id. The Court did, however, construe the State's appeal as a petition for writ of certiorari and accepted jurisdiction. Id.; but see id. at 9-10 (Taylor, J., concurring in part and dissenting in part, for argument supporting State's right to appeal).

Reaching the merits, the Court found that the juvenile's plea suffered from "multiple infirmities":

(1) Juvenile not placed under oath;
(2) Juvenile not questioned about her understanding of the plea agreement;
(3) Juvenile not questioned about the possible dispositions or consequences;
(4) Juvenile not asked whether she understood rights being waived pursuant to the plea.

Id. at 9. Under these circumstances, the Court found "the colloquy was so brief, it was almost nonexistent." Id. Also pertinent, the Court held, was the fact that the juvenile demonstrated prejudice as it was established that she would not have entered plea had counsel properly advised her as to expunction. Id. Further, because the motion was filed within 1-year of discovering the error, the juvenile's claim was timely filed. Id. Finding the trial court did not depart from the essential requirements of the law, the Court denied the State's petition for writ of certiorari. Id.

This case demonstrates the importance of fully understanding all consequences surrounding plea agreements. It is vital that before entering a plea, a defendant discuss with his or her attorney not only the direct consequences (such as incarceration or probation), but also the indirect consequences (revocation of licenses, permanency of criminal record, etc). These are all considerations that should not be weighed lightly. In the event that counsel did not discuss these, or improperly advised (as was the case here), postconviction relief may be available.

Loren Rhoton, P.A.
Postconviction Attorneys

412 East Madison Street
Suite 1111
Tampa, Florida 33602
Tel: 813-226-3138
Fax: 813-221-2182
Email:
lorenrhoton@rhotonpostconviction.com
rsydejko@rhotonpostconviction.com

- Direct Appeals
- Belated Appeals
- Rule 3.850 Motions
- Illegal Sentence Corrections
- Rule 9.141 Petitions
- Federal Habeas Corpus Petitions
- Clemency Petitions and Waivers

The Florida Postconviction Journal publishes up to four times per year. This Journal provides resources for information affecting prisoners, their families, friends, loved ones, and the general public of the State of Florida. Promoting skilled access to the court system for indigent prisoners is a primary goal of this publication. Due to the volume of mail that is received, not all correspondence can be returned. If you would like return of materials, please enclose a postage-paid and pre-addressed envelope. This publication is not meant to be a substitute for legal or other professional advice. The material addressed in the Journal should not be relied upon as authoritative and may not contain sufficient information to deal with specific legal issues.

The Florida Postconviction Journal
a publication of Loren Rhoton, P.A.
412 East Madison Street
Suite 1111
Tampa, FL 33602

CHANGE SERVICE REQUESTED

Name
Institution
Street Address
City, State, Zip

The Florida Postconviction Journal

Volume 1
Issue 4

a quarterly publication of Loren Rhoton, P.A.

Fall 2011

"He that can have patience, can have what he will."

~Benjamin Franklin

This issue of *The Florida Postconviction Journal* is a combination Summer/Fall issue. While we strive to provide a quarterly publication, the writing and publication of the FPJ is all done by Ryan Sydejko, the staff of my office, and myself. As a result, occasionally an issue of FPJ may not come out right at the beginning of each quarter. We strive to provide helpful information to Florida inmates and do not wish to merely load the newsletter with filler. Therefore, sometimes we may get behind a little bit in our publication schedule. This only occurs because we want to make sure that we are providing something of value to our readers. We hope that the quality of the information and advice in FPJ more than makes up for any small delay in publication.

If you find the information in our newsletter to be helpful, please spread the word and let others know about the free subscription for Florida prisoners. If you would like to see articles on specific legal issues in our upcoming newsletters, write us with your ideas. We obviously will not be able to address every request (nor will we be able to respond to every letter). But, we will do our best to disseminate information that our readers will find valuable. And, finally, please let us know what you like (or don't like) about our newsletter. We want to know if our publication is one that our readers will want to continue to receive. Particularly relevant comments may even be included in future issues of FPJ.

So, there you have it. We apologize for the delay in our latest newsletter and want to hear from our readers. Hopefully you find our latest issue to be informative and helpful. If so, please share it with others and spread the word about FPJ.

Loren Rhoton

Obtaining Copies of Evidence & Public Records From Uncooperative State Agencies

In Parish v. State, 2011 WL 1775740 (Fla. 4th DCA 2011) the Fourth District Court of Appeal addressed the issue of an inmate's difficulty in obtaining copies of a document that was admitted into evidence at trial. Following his conviction, the defendant sought a copy of the Miranda rights waiver form. Id. at *1. Parish began by serving multiple §119 public record requests on the Office of the State Attorney, the Clerk of the Circuit Court, and the Office of the Public Defender. Id. The Clerk's Office responded that it possessed a copy, and would deliver same upon payment of copying expenses. Id. Parish remitted payment, but the Clerk's Office responded that it, in fact, did not possess the Miranda rights waiver form. Id.

Utilizing the proper channels, Parish then pursued a Petition for Writ of Mandamus, requesting the Circuit Court to direct the State of Florida to perform it's statutory obligations and produce the requested document. Id. The State responded, arguing that it did not possess the document; instead, it argued, the Clerk of Court possessed the form. Id. Therefore, the petition should be dismissed as it was not sought against the proper party. Id. Adopting this rationale, the Circuit Court denied relief, directing Parish to take his document request up with the Clerk of Court (which Parish had obviously tried, and failed). Id.

Appeal was taken to the Fourth DCA, which reversed and remanded. Id. at *2. The DCA found two errors: (1) the State's response alleging the Clerk had the form was unsworn, and therefore could not conclusively refute Parish's assertions; and (2) the trial court should have granted Parish leave to include the Clerk of Court as a party to the Petition. Id. at *2. In dicta, the DCA also wrote that the Clerk should either turn over the form, or prove at an evidentiary hearing that it no longer possesses the form.

About Loren Rhoton, P.A.

Loren Rhoton, P.A. is a law firm that focuses exclusively on postconviction actions and inmate issues. The mission of Loren Rhoton, P.A. is to ensure that justice is accomplished in each and every case the firm undertakes. The firm's area of practice ranges from direct criminal appeals and postconviction actions to assisting inmates in dealing with the Florida Department of Corrections. Loren Rhoton, P.A., is a small firm, consisting of Mr. Loren D. Rhoton and Mr. Ryan J. Sydejko. The firm strives to keep a small caseload in order to give each case the individual attention it deserves. We are not a volume business. We do not accept every case that is presented to the firm for representation. A thorough review of any potential case will be conducted before the firm undertakes full representation. If you wish to have your case reviewed for representation, please contact Loren Rhoton for more information. If inquiring about representation, please do not send any materials to the firm that you wish to have returned to you.

Loren D. Rhoton, Esq.

Loren D. Rhoton is an attorney in private practice with the law office of Loren Rhoton, P.A., in Tampa, Florida. Mr. Rhoton graduated from the University of Toledo College of Law and has been a member in good standing with The Florida Bar since his admission to practice in 1995. The exclusive focus of Mr. Rhoton's practice is dedicated to assisting Florida inmates with their criminal appeal/postconviction cases.

Mr. Rhoton is a member of The Florida Bar's Appellate Division. He is also a member of the U.S. District Court, in and for the Middle and Northern Districts of Florida. Mr. Rhoton is licensed to practice before the U.S. Court of Appeals for the 11th Circuit and is also certified to practice before the U.S. Supreme Court. Mr. Rhoton regularly practices before Federal District Courts and the U.S. Court of Appeals for the 11th Circuit.

Mr. Rhoton typically deals with clients who have lengthy prison sentences. Mr. Rhoton has investigated and pursued hundreds of postconviction cases. He has practiced in all phases of the Florida Judicial System, all the way from misdemeanor county courts up to the Florida Supreme Court. Additionally, Mr. Rhoton has been directly responsible for amendments to Florida Rule of Criminal Procedure 3.850 (the main vehicle for most postconviction actions). Mr. Rhoton is appointed by the Florida Supreme Court to the Florida Criminal Rules Steering Committee, Subcommittee on Postconviction Relief, which is focused on rewriting Florida Rule of Criminal Procedure 3.850. Mr. Rhoton works on said subcommittee with judges and other governmental officials in an effort to improve the administration and execution of postconviction proceedings. Mr. Rhoton's role on said committee has been to advocate for changes that will be beneficial to postconviction litigants (inmates).

For over a decade, Mr. Rhoton authored a bimonthly article, *Post Conviction Corner*, for Florida Prison Legal Perspectives. Selected articles from *Post Conviction Corner* have been compiled and printed in a legal self-help book, *Postconviction Relief for the Florida Prisoner*. Mr. Rhoton also served on the Board of Directors of the Florida Prisoner's Legal Aid Organization, Inc.

Ryan J. Sydejko, Esq.

Ryan J. Sydejko is an attorney with the law office of Loren Rhoton, P.A. His practice focuses primarily on postconviction matters for those incarcerated throughout the State of Florida. He has argued cases before many circuit courts and District Courts of Appeal and has several published opinions. Mr. Sydejko has also presented cases to the Supreme Court of Florida and the U.S. District Courts for the Middle and Northern Districts of Florida.

Mr. Sydejko graduated from the University of Minnesota with a degree in political science and attended the University of Tulsa College of Law. As a student, he authored a law review article entitled: "International Influence on Democracy: How Terrorism Exploited a Deteriorating Fourth Amendment." The article, exploring how domestic terrorist threats have reshaped everyday law enforcement procedures, was published in the Spring 2006 edition of the Wayne State University Law School Journal of Law in Society. Mr. Sydejko also wrote articles for the Florida Prison Legal Perspectives. Mr. Sydejko is a member in good standing with the Florida Bar and is qualified to practice in all Florida state courts, as well as the Federal District Courts for the Middle and Northern Districts of Florida.

The Florida Postconviction Journal

Volume 1
Issue 4

a quarterly publication of Loren Rhoton, P.A.

Notable Firm Cases

Dames v. State, 773 So.2d 563 (Fla. 2d DCA 2000) – Improper summary denial of Rule 3.850 Motion reversed & remanded for evidentiary hearing.

Dames v. State, 807 So.2d 756 (Fla. 2d DCA 2002) – First Degree Murder conviction vacated & new trial granted due to ineffective counsel

Battle v. State, 710 So.2d 628 (Fla. 2d DCA 1998) – Improper Habitual Felony Offender Sentence on violation of probation reversed & remanded for resentencing

Mitchell v. State, 734 So.2d 1067 (Fla. 1st DCA 1999) - counsel can render ineffective assistance for failure to argue boarded-up structure is not a 'dwelling' under arson statute

Caban v. State, 9 So.3d 50 (Fla. 5th DCA 2009) – counsel can be ineffective for failing to object to improper impeachment of defense expert witnesses in Shaken Baby Syndrome case

Graff v. State, 846 So.2d 582 (Fla. 2d DCA 2003) – attorney's misadvice as to potential sentence can amount to ineffective assistance of counsel sufficient to justify withdrawal of plea.

Easley v. State, 742 So.2d 463 (Fla. 2d DCA 1999) – counsel can render ineffective assistance for failure to investigate insanity defense.

Campbell v. State, 16 So.3d 316 (Fla. 2d DCA 2009) – Manifest Injustice – summary denial of Rule 3.800 motion to correct illegal sentence reversed & remanded on manifest injustice grounds.

Thompson v. State, 987 So.2d 727 (Fla. 4th DCA 2008) – Reversal of Life Sentences – entitled to de novo resentencing upon correction of improper consecutive life sentences for murder and burglary.

Williams v. State, 777 So.2d 947 (Fla. 2000) – Right to Belated Postconviction Motion – if post-conviction counsel fails to timely file Rule 3.850 Motion, defendant has right to file belated appeal.

Parker v. State, 977 So.2d 671 (Fla. 4th DCA 2008) – Sentence reversed & remanded for resentencing due to judicial vindictiveness

Challenging Habitual Offender Sentences: Rule 3.800 or 3.850?

In White v. State, 60 So.3d 1101 (Fla. 5th DCA 2011), Latarsa White challenged her habitualized sentences pursuant to Florida Rule of Criminal Procedure 3.800.

White had previously entered a plea of no contest to robbery and grand theft, and was sentenced as an habitual felony offender ("HFO"). Id. at 1102. Imposition of the HFO status came as the product of a stipulation between the State and White. Id. Following completion of her 48-month term of incarceration, White's probation was revoked after a violation and she was sentenced to 30-years imprisonment. Id. White's postconviction challenges began as she subsequently filed a Rule 3.850 motion, challenging counsel's performance at the violation of probation proceeding. Id. Said motion was denied, and affirmed on appeal. Id.

White then filed a Rule 3.800(a) motion alleging the HFO designation was improper as her prior felonies (possession of cocaine) did not qualify as proper predicate offenses. Id.

The District Court began by noting that typically, a Rule 3.800 Motion to Correct Illegal Sentence is the proper vehicle for addressing the lack of predicate felonies for HFO designations. Id. at 1103. In most situations, it's clear from the face of the record. Id. For example, the Court can simply view the file to determine whether: (a) documents exist to prove prior felony convictions; and (b) whether said convictions are of the proper variety to support an HFO designation.

This case, however, was different. Under these circumstances, the Court held, White should have challenged the designation under Rule 3.850. Id. Because White previously stipulated to the HFO designation, the State was not required to produce documentation proving the predicate offenses. Id. As a result, the trial court's record is silent (lacks documentation) as to White's claims. Because White cannot show, as clear from the face of the record, her designation is improper, White should have made this claim in her Rule 3.850 motion so the Court could hold an evidentiary hearing to accept evidence regarding the existence of prior felonies.

To Order Back Issues of
The Florida Postconviction Journal:

Please send a check or money order made payable to Loren Rhoton, P.A. in the amount of $3.50 per issue. Also, please designate the Volume and Issue number of each issue desired (found on the first page of each issue). Allow two to three weeks for delivery.

Florida Supreme Court Limits Previously Accorded Constitutional Protections

by Loren D. Rhoton

On June 16, 2011, the Florida Supreme Court (F.S.Ct.), in State v. Powell, 36 F.L.W. S264 (Fla. 2011) [Powell I] reversed its previous ruling in State v. Powell, 998 So.2d 531 (Fla.2008) [Powell II], and limited the Miranda protections that it had previously afforded Florida arrestees. In Powell I, F.S.Ct. found that the Miranda rights read by Tampa Police to arrestees were unconstitutional, in violation of the Fifth Amendment of the U.S. Constitution, because said rights advised that an arrestee had the right to a lawyer prior to counseling, and the right to consult a lawyer during questioning, but did not properly inform the arrestees that they had the right to the presence of counsel during interrogation. Subsequent to the issuance of Powell I, the issue was appealed to the Supreme Court of the United States (S.C.O.T.U.S), which found that the Fifth Amendment does not require a warning that an arrestee has the right to the presence of an attorney during questioning when the arrestee is otherwise advised that he has the right to consult with an attorney before and during questioning.

Upon remand from S.C.O.T.U.S., the F.S.Ct. reconsidered its ruling in Powell I. Powell II concluded that its previous ruling was based entirely on federal constitutional principles and, further, that the Miranda warnings did not run afoul of any Florida Constitutional protections. As such, the holding in Powell I has now been reversed and the Miranda warnings in question are once again considered to be proper.

It is important that inmates considering seeking postconviction relief evaluate whether Powell

II has any effect on their case. I always like to advise inmates to seek postconviction relief if it is available and it is prudent to do so. However, there are circumstances where a postconviction litigant can put himself in a worse situation by having a conviction overturned. Powell II creates such a concern and all postconviction litigants should evaluate Powell II's effect on their cases. It is possible that statements that were previously suppressed at trial, as per Powell I, may now come back to haunt a defendant as admissible evidence. In other words, just because a statement to police was previously inadmissible (as per Powell I), the exact same statement may end up being admissible (and, thus strengthening the State's case at retrial) if postconviction relief is sought and a new trial is granted.

For some, Powell II could possibly strengthen the State's case at retrial, or, conceivably, give the State additional facts with which it could even pursue enhanced charges. For others, Powell II may have no real effect on the strength of the State's case on retrial. Nevertheless, if suppressed statements were an issue in your case, it is advisable to review the Powell cases, determine what effect (if any) they may have on your case, and then act as is in the best interest of your case. In some situations, this may mean abandoning what previously seemed to be a strong postconviction motion. In other cases it may just be an additional consideration to be aware of. And, in some cases, it may make no difference whatsoever. But, it is better to be aware of Powell II now than to be surprised by its effect when it is too late.

Hearsay Evidence & VOP Hearings

In order to demonstrate a violation of probation, the State must prove by a greater weight of the evidence a willful and substantial violation of a condition of probation. Van Wagner v. State, 677 So.2d 314, 316 (Fla. 1st DCA 1996). Hearsay evidence is typically admissible in order to meet that burden. But, in order to prove a violation occurred due to commission of a new offense, direct non-hearsay evidence is required. Melton v. State, 36 Fla. L. Weekly D1354.

In Melton, a hearing was held on whether the probationer violated by smoking marijuana. Melton denied smoking marijuana. The probation officer who

administered the drug test did not testify. The only evidence presented against the probationer was the testimony of a different probation officer who had no personal knowledge of the drug test. While the State conceded the evidence insufficient to support a VOP, the court revoked probation anyways. The probationer was also violated for failing to report.

The First District Court of Appeal reversed and remanded, reiterating that VOP's based upon commission of a new offense must be supported by direct, non-hearsay evidence. The DCA struck the revocation of the marijuana allegation, but left intact the failure to report, of which the testifying probation officer did have personal knowledge.

The Florida Postconviction Journal

Volume 1
Issue 4

a quarterly publication of Loren Rhoton, P.A.

page 5 of 10

Reversible Error When Bailiff Improperly Communicates with Jury During Deliberations

by Ryan J. Sydejko

In <u>Natan v. State</u>, 2011 WL 1565994 (Fla. 2d DCA 2011), the Second District Court of Appeal was confronted with alleged improper conduct of a courtroom bailiff during jury deliberations. The facts revealed that as the jury was about to render a verdict, a juror informed the bailiff that a piece of evidence sent back with the jury had been mislabeled. <u>Id.</u> at *1. Although the piece of evidence bore the proper tag for Natan's case, it also apparently bore a tag for another, unrelated case. <u>Id.</u> Upon delivery of the evidence to the courtroom, the bailiff informed the Assistant State Attorney of the issue. <u>Id.</u> But, the bailiff also advised that "he had taken care of the situation, the ASA had some help, and not to bring it up." <u>Id.</u>

Several days later, after a judgment of guilt had been rendered by the jury, that same ASA wrote a letter to both the trial judge and Natan's counsel disclosing the bailiff's comments. <u>Id.</u> The ASA added that he personally knew the bailiff and believed his comments to be in jest, but felt a duty to disclose the comments. <u>Id.</u>

In reversing Natan's convictions for aggravated stalking and arson, the Second DCA cited the Florida Supreme Court's "per se reversible error rule when a bailiff has unsupervised communications with a jury." <u>Id.</u>; see also <u>State v. Merricks</u>, 831 So.2d 156, 161 (2002). This is significant, as it is unknown whether the bailiff actually improperly communicated with the jury. The bailiff's comments created a reasonable inference that words relating to the case at hand had been improperly exchanged with the jury. Based on the bailiff's statement to the ASA "that he had taken care of the situation, the ASA had some help, and not to bring it up," the Second DCA felt compelled to reverse the convictions. <u>Natan</u>, 2011 WL 1565994 at *1.

Support Services for Inmates & Their Families Available

If you have a suggestion for a group or inmate resource that should be listed in our newsletter, please contact us with the information and we will share any helpful information in future issues.

Innocence Project of Florida.
1100 East Park Ave.
Tallahassee, FL, 32301
Phone: (850) 561-6767
   Assists inmates with postconviction DNA innocence cases and helps exonerees in obtaining compensation for wrongful convictions.

R.I.S.E. (Relations of Inmates Supporting Each-Other).
23184 Allen Avenue,
Port Charlotte, FL, 33980
Phone: (941)421-6907
Contact: Candy Kendrick
Email: RISEFLORIDA@Yahoo.com
   Offers support to the friends and families of Florida inmates. Programs include a carpool connection, Books for Inmates, a Christmas toy drive for children of inmates, assistance to out-of-state families visiting Florida inmates, new visitor seminars, and a newsletter.

Florida Legal Services. www.floridalegalhelp.org
2121 Delta Blvd., Tallahassee, FL, 32303
Phone: (904) 385-7900
   Provides referrals in civil matters.

Prisontalk.com. An Internet community/forum that provides general information and networking for families of inmates. Also, has Florida specific forum that addresses issues ranging from dealing with the D.O.C. to coping with incarceration.

Florida Justice Institute, Inc.
4320 Bank of America Tower
100 S.E. Second Street
Miami, FL, 33131
Phone: (305) 358-2081
Contact: Randall C. Berg, Jr.
Email: rcberg@floridajusticeinstitute.org
   Handles civil-rights cases regarding conditions in prisons and jails; advocates and lobbies on behalf of prisoners.

To Subscribe or Change Your Mailing Address
to *The Florida Postconviction Journal:*

The *Florida Postconviction Journal* is currently being provided, free of charge, to Florida inmates who are interested in receiving the helpful advice and information contained in the newsletter. If you wish to have your name added to the newsletter's mailing list, please fill out the form below and mail it to Loren Rhoton, P.A., 412 East Madison Street, Suite 1111, Tampa, FL 33062. For non-inmates interested in subscribing to the newsletter, please forward a money order in the amount of $25 for a one-year subscription.

Please Check One:

☐ New Subscriber

☐ Change of Address

Name _____ DC# _____

Institution Name and Street Address _____

City _____ State _____ Zip _____

Did Law Enforcement Officer Misunderstand the Word "No"?

In Black v. State, 59 So.3d 340 (Fla. 4th DCA 2011), the Court reviewed a suppression issue pertaining to statements made following allegedly invoked Miranda rights. Black, the defendant, was charged and convicted of two counts of first-degree murder. Id. at 342. On the evening of his arrest, officers placed Black in a video-monitored interrogation room. Id. Officers provided Miranda warnings, which included the following exchange:

> Officer: Knowing and understanding your rights as I have explained them to you, are you willing to answer my questions without an attorney?
>
> Black: No.

Id. at 343. The officer then instructed Black to sign and date the form, after which Black provided a lengthy and detrimental video-recorded statement. Id. After a suppression hearing, the trial court held that the officer simply "did not comprehend Black's response of 'no'" and that the officer had not slept in a while. Id. at 344. Following a conviction on both counts and imposition of two life sentences, Black appealed, alleging the trial court erred in denying the motion to suppress. Id. at 342.

The Fourth District Court of Appeal overturned Black's convictions and sentences, holding that the trial court's order was not supported by competent and substantial evidence. Id. at 344. Notably, the DCA found that no officer testified to being tired or "missing" Black's responses (as the trial court held). Id. In fact, the officer specifically testified that he "clearly understood Black's responses." Id.

An important aspect of this case is the fact that Black's interrogation was video-recorded and played, in its entirety at the suppression hearing. Cases involving invocation of Miranda rights are difficult to win on appeal as the standard of review is quite high. Appellate courts are very deferential to the factual findings of lower courts as those lower courts are much better situated to evaluate live testimony and witness credibility. In a situation where video-recorders catch much of the testimony, however, and a DVD copy is available to the appellate court, a "much less deferential standard" will be utilized. Id. at 344.

In this case, the DCA was afforded the luxury of a video-recorded set of facts that "illuminate a bright line thereby permitting a clear and simple application of the exclusionary rule." Id. at 347.

The DCA held that there was but one "inescapable conclusion." Id. Because Black unequivocally invoked his right to counsel by answering 'no', and because the officer testified that he clearly understood Black's responses, it had no choice but to reverse Black's convictions and order a new trial. Id.

The Florida Postconviction Journal

Volume 1
Issue 4

a quarterly publication of Loren Rhoton, P.A.   page 7 of 10

Pro-Se Inmate Filings and the Rebuttable Mailbox Rule

An important aspect of filing *pro se* documents while incarcerated is the Mailbox Rule. The Mailbox Rule simply states that a document is deemed filed the moment it is handed to Department of Corrections officials. *See* Haag v. State, 591 So.2d 614, 617 (Fla. 1992). The reasoning behind this is that incarcerated individuals entrust processing and timely delivery to a third-party (DOC officials) and have no further control over when and how the mail is actually sent. Id. For example, an institution may have incredibly slow outgoing mail, which could cause a filing to sit for days, meanwhile the period of limitations expires, to no fault of the inmate filer. The Mailbox Rule was developed to address this.

An concern has arisen, at least with some, regarding how to determine exactly which day the inmate turned over the document to DOC officials for purposes of mailing. That brings us to the case of Thompson v. State, 36 Fla. L. Weekly D968 (Fla. 2d DCA 2011).

In Thompson, Thompson's two-year period of limitations was set to expire on May 15, 2010. Id. at *1. Thompson certified that he placed his postconviction motion into the hands of DOC officials on May 12, 2010; but, the motion was not received by the Clerk of Court until June 16, 2010. Id. The trial court dismissed the motion as untimely. Id. (the motion was also denied as successive, but that is not pertinent to this discussion). The Second District Court of Appeal reversed the denial, finding that Thompson's pleading was, in fact, timely. Id. The majority reasoned that a document containing a certificate of service showing the date the document was placed into DOC hands is, for all intents and purposes, deemed filed with the Court on that same date. Id.; *see also* Thompson v. State, 761 So.2d 324, 326 (Fla. 2000). This holding, however, is not absolute.

Judge Villanti, concurring with the majority, added this caveat: the inmate's date certification is merely a presumption, and is therefore rebuttable by the State. Id. at *2. Judge Villanti then went on to instruct the State on how to make such challenges, by focusing mainly on prison mail logs. Id. Villanti also issued a warning to inmates who may wish to be dishonest, citing penalties for contempt of court and charges of perjury. Id.

The bottom line is to remember the importance of including certifications of when the mail was placed into DOC hands. Some institutions even use date-stamps requiring inmate signatures or initials when outgoing mail leaves an inmate's custody. Such a measure may allay Judge Villanti's worries while ensuring inmate's filings are not unjustly rejected by the Courts as untimely.

DCA Calls Out Circuit Court Judges for Repeated Improper Denials of Postconviction Motion

As the Second District Court of Appeal sees it, D'Angelo LaVelle Dixon is an impatient man. Dixon v. State, 60 So.3d 1179 (Fla. 2d DCA 2011). Dixon was convicted of aggravated battery with a deadly weapon, robbery with a firearm, and attempted first-degree murder. Id. at 1180. While his direct appeal was pending, Dixon filed his first postconviction motion in May 2005. Id. The motion was filed so quickly, Dixon did not even know the name of the lawyer appointed to represent him on direct appeal. Id. In September 2005, Judge Frederick Hardt dismissed the motion due to lack of jurisdiction. Id. Dixon did not appeal. Id. Then in October 2005, Judge Hardt "inexplicably" entered an order staying the dismissal of the postconviction proceeding. Id. A year later, the mandate from Dixon's direct appeal was issued, in November 2006. Id.

Judge Bruce Kyle then picked up the stayed postconviction proceeding, and denied it, holding that the issue should have been raised on direct appeal. Id. Dixon timely appealed Judge Kyle's order, but voluntarily dismissed it prior to a DCA ruling. Id.

Dixon then filed a proceeding in the DCA, alleging ineffectiveness of appellate counsel for failing to raise the issue. Id. The DCA denied the claim in November 2007. Id.

In November 2008, Dixon then filed a motion for postconviction relief, alleging seven grounds for relief. Id. A month later, the State's two-page response requesting denial of the motion based upon successiveness, since Dixon already filed one such motion. Id. Almost two-years later, In August 2010, Judge Christine Greider denied Dixon's motion for postconviction relief. Id. at *2.

The District Court, obviously unhappy it had to deal with Dixon's case, again, took great effort to pinpoint each error made by the circuit court judges.

First, Judge Greider attached only a two-page document to her order, which obviously does not clearly refute all seven of Dixon's claims, as required under Rule 3.850. Second, the attachments do not support most of Judge Greider's factual and procedural representations. Third, Judge Greider grossly miscalculated the period of limitations (Rule 3.850 proscribes a two-year period, Judge Greider gave Dixon only one day).

Judge Greider also likely incorrectly found the motion successive, since Judge Hardt dismissed it as premature several years earlier. Id. at 1181. Besides the uncommon use of the circuit judge's names in the opinion, the DCA closed with the following:

> "In the twenty-one months that the November 2008 motion was pending below, we are inclined to believe that the trial court could have reached a better reasoned decision in accordance with the rules of procedure and due process. We have no way to judge whether Mr. Dixon has a claim worthy of serious consideration, but we know it has not received such consideration."

Id. at 1181. The DCA went on to note in a footnote, that Dixon's "flurry" of additional filings since Judge Greider's denial may also be affected by this ruling. Id. at fn. 5.

This case is noteworthy for a couple reasons. First, opinions such as this are fairly uncommon. DCA's do not usually call-out circuit court judges by name. In a way, the DCA nearly issued Judge Greider a public reprimand for her long-delayed, yet wholly inadequate disposition of Dixon's case. Secondly, this case is a useful tutorial in how not to begin the postconviction process. Even viable claims could get procedurally barred by using the wrong vehicle or filing at the wrong time, as Dixon nearly did. Dixon is fortunate that the Second DCA took the time to sort through his procedural labyrinth. Obviously, Judge Greider was not.

Quotable:

Judge Altenbernd, of the Second District Court of Appeal, offered this tidbit in Nieminski v. State, 2011 WL 1599572 (Fla. 2d DCA 2011):

"It is undisputed that Mr. Nieminski, his girlfriend, his horse, and his three friendly dogs had been living at this grow house for approximately a month before the execution of the search warrant. Mr. Nieminski was not a trespasser on this property; he was both working and living full time at this location. We conclude that these undisputed facts, in addition to providing a solid foundation for a country-western song, are sufficient to satisfy Mr. Nieminski's threshold burden under the Katz analysis . . ."

Cell Phones and the Police: Where Will the Searching of Web-Enabled Phones End?

by Ryan J. Sydejko

In <u>Smallwood v. State</u>, 36 Fla. L. Weekly D911 (Fla. 1st DCA 2011), the First District Court of Appeal tackled the developing area of warrantless searches of electronic storage devices. As frequent readers of *The Florida Postconviction Journal*, you know that the issue of warrantless searches is governed by the Fourth Amendment which proscribes the right "to be secure in their persons, houses, papers, and effects, against unreasonable searches and seizures. U.S. Const. Amend IV. As a *very* general rule, searches are reasonable only if officers obtain a warrant first. <u>Coolidge v. New Hampshire</u>, 403 U.S. 443, 449-453 (1971). There are, however, a litany of "specifically established and well-delineated exceptions to the warrant requirement." <u>Katz v. U.S.</u>, 389 U.S. 347 (1967). For the purposes of this discussion, one such exception is the search incident to lawful arrest and the search of all items and containers within that person's reach. *See* <u>U.S. v. Robinson</u>, 414 U.S. 218 (1973). It is <u>Robinson</u> upon which the Court relied in upholding the officer's search in <u>Smallwood</u>.

In <u>Robinson</u>, the Supreme Court reiterated the legality of searches incident to lawful arrest, and further expounded on the principle, allowing officers to search any containers found upon the person, even without any "additional justification." <u>Id.</u> at 234. What this meant, effectively, is that officers could search locked luggage, bags, containers, etc, regardless of whether they potentially housed evidence of the purported offense. <u>Id.</u> This issue has become extremely hot as electronic devices, with near infinite storage capabilities, are now being routinely searched by law enforcement. In the instant case, Smallwood was arrested and his cell phone searched. <u>Smallwood</u> at *1. The officer justified the search, testifying that he looked at Smallwood's phone "too see if he took any pictures" that would "relate to the crime" because he "knew people sometimes do that." <u>Id.</u>

Smallwood challenged the legality of the search, giving rise to the instant case. Without going through the rather extensive history of searches incident to arrest, the District Court ultimately upheld the search. <u>Id.</u> (if you are interested in this principle, or believe it may have bearing on your case, you are highly encouraged to read the <u>Smallwood</u> case in its entirety; the Court begins the discussion with the very origin of the principal in *Chimel v. California*, 395 U.S. 752 (1969) and continues through the latest line of cases, including <u>U.S. v. Finley</u>, 477 F.3d 250 (5th Cir. 2007)).

Article I, section 12, of the Florida Constitution specifically provides that the right against unreasonable search and seizure as granted under the Florida Constitution "shall be construed in conformity with the Fourth Amendment to the United States Constitution, as interpreted by the United States Supreme Court." By doing so, the Florida Constitution actually removes the ability to decide such cases from Florida courts, and places them firmly into the hands of the nine United States Supreme Court justices. This process may work for some, but cases typically take years to finally reach the Supreme Court and can lag far behind newly minted legal issues; i.e. the search of ever expanding electronic devices. For example, in resolving the issue in <u>Smallwood</u>, the Florida Supreme Court applied the ruling in <u>Robinson</u>, a case from 1973. It would be hard to believe that the <u>Robinson</u> court, in 1973, foresaw applicability of their physical containers holding to tiny, electronic storage devices that can contain near infinite volumes of data and personal information.

Therein lies the problem. While a cell phone containing photographs actually has the photographs stored on it's memory (similar to a photo stashed in locked luggage), data is increasingly not being stored on the actual device. What, then, becomes of an email application? Emails that have been viewed on the device are then stored in the flash storage, but unviewed emails have yet to be downloaded from the server. From the <u>Smallwood</u> Court's holding, we can infer that all previously viewed emails are fair game since they are actually stored within the container, or phone, itself. If, however, the officer clicks on the email application, which then automatically downloads all new email, can the officer view it without a warrant? Further, what do we make of documents and photographs that are stored in the 'cloud', but are accessible from the device? Can the officer use the cloud application to gain access to those items? It could take years for constantly developing issues, such as those eluded to above, appear before the United States Supreme Court. In the meantime, Florida courts must rely on out-moded and out-dated interpretations based on the storage of physical items inside larger containers from cases decided in the 1960's.

The First DCA did certify the issue to the Florida Supreme Court, so stay tuned!

Loren Rhoton, P.A.

Postconviction Attorneys

412 East Madison Street
Suite 1111
Tampa, Florida 33602
Tel: 813-226-3138
Fax: 813-221-2182
Email:
lorenrhoton@rhotonpostconviction.com
rsydejko@rhotonpostconviction.com

- Direct Appeals
- Belated Appeals
- Rule 3.850 Motions
- Illegal Sentence Corrections
- Rule 9.141 Petitions
- Federal Habeas Corpus Petitions
- Clemency Petitions and Waivers

The Florida Postconviction Journal publishes up to four times per year. This Journal provides resources for information affecting prisoners, their families, friends, loved ones, and the general public of the State of Florida. Promoting skilled access to the court system for indigent prisoners is a primary goal of this publication. Due to the volume of mail that is received, not all correspondence can be returned. If you would like return of materials, please enclose a postage-paid and pre-addressed envelope. This publication is not meant to be a substitute for legal or other professional advice. The material addressed in the Journal should not be relied upon as authoritative and may not contain sufficient information to deal with specific legal issues.

The Florida Postconviction Journal
a publication of Loren Rhoton, P.A.
412 East Madison Street
Suite 1111
Tampa, FL 33602

CHANGE SERVICE REQUESTED

Name
Institution
Street Address
City, State, Zip

The Florida Postconviction Journal

Volume 2
Issue 1

a quarterly publication of Loren Rhoton, P.A.

Spring 2012

Florida Drug Trafficking Statute Unconstitutional?

In one of the recent major postconviction developments in Florida, the United States District Court for the Middle District of Florida held that Florida's drug trafficking statute, Florida Statute §893.13, is facially unconstitutional as a violation of the Due Process Clause of the U.S. Constitution. Shelton v. Florida, 802 F.Supp.2d 1289 (2011), found that the trafficking statute amounts to a strict liability crime because it eliminates *mens rea* (guilty knowledge) as an element of drug distribution offenses. The potential effect of Shelton is to invalidate thousands of trafficking convictions in Florida. And, predictably, some of the Florida District Courts have scrambled to try to invalidate Shelton. *See*, Flagg v. State, 74 So.3d 138

(Fla.1st DCA 2011) and, Maestas v. State, 76 So.3d 991 (Fla. 4th DCA 2011).

I have received numerous letters from inmates about the status of Shelton in Florida. Currently, the Florida Supreme Court is considering the question in State v. Adkins, (case #SC11-1878), and an opinion is expected soon. Oral argument was heard in Adkins on December 6, 2011, and as of this date, the Florida Supreme Court has not yet issued its decision. Hopefully, by the printing of the next issue FPJ, the Florida Supreme Court will have ruled (and, of course, agreed with Shelton). Along with many others, we will be keeping a close eye on Shelton, and will alert FPJ readers of the result.

Loren D. Rhoton

Police Officer's Videotaped Statements: Hearsay or Verbal Acts?

Not all out-of-court statements are created equal. In State v. Holland, 76 So.3d 1032 (Fla. 4th DCA 2012), the Court was presented with a situation that involved a DUI stop, refused breath test, administration of field sobriety exercises and the conversations between the officer and Holland. Id. at 1033. One officer videotaped the encounter while another officer administered the tests and participated in the conversations. Id. The State chose not to call the officer whom conducted the videotaping. Id. The defense immediately moved to suppress the videotape based on the Confrontation Clause. Id. The State countered, arguing that the videotape was not hearsay, and, even if it was, the tape was nontestimonial. Id. The trial court granted the motion to suppress the videotape. Id. at 1034.

The appellate court began by holding that a refusal to submit to sobriety testing is admissible under the implied consent law, regardless of the videotape issue. Id.

The court next examined Holland's statements caught on videotape. Id. The court quickly found that Holland's statements constituted admissions of a party

opponent, a clear exception to the hearsay rule under Fla. Stat. § 90.803(18)(a). Id.

The court next examined whether the officer's statements caught on video were admissible. The officer's directives during the sobriety exercises were both verbal and non-verbal, meaning the officer was likely giving verbal instructions on how to perform the tasks while simultaneously demonstrating how they were to be done. *See* id. The court held that the officer's statements were verbal acts: "utterance[s] of an operative fact that give rise to legal consequences." Id. Verbal acts are not hearsay because they are not admitted to prove the truth of the matter asserted, but rather to prove that statements were actually made.

While a finding that spoken words are verbal acts may appear to be judicial acrobatics, it is an important distinction to be aware of, especially in the postconviction context when rooting out meritless claims is critical to presentation of the motion. Always be mindful that an issue that appears obvious (i.e. that words are not acts) may in fact not be an issue at all.

<u>About Loren Rhoton, P.A.</u>

Loren Rhoton, P.A. is a law firm that focuses exclusively on postconviction actions and inmate issues. The mission of Loren Rhoton, P.A. is to ensure that justice is accomplished in each and every case the firm undertakes. The firm's area of practice ranges from direct criminal appeals and postconviction actions to assisting inmates in dealing with the Florida Department of Corrections. Loren Rhoton, P.A., is a small firm, consisting of Mr. Loren D. Rhoton and Mr. Ryan J. Sydejko. The firm strives to keep a small caseload in order to give each case the individual attention it deserves. We are not a volume business. We do not accept every case that is presented to the firm for representation. A thorough review of any potential case will be conducted before the firm undertakes full representation. If you wish to have your case reviewed for representation, please contact Loren Rhoton for more information. If inquiring about representation, please do not send any materials to the firm that you wish to have returned to you.

Loren D. Rhoton, Esq.

Loren D. Rhoton is an attorney in private practice with the law office of Loren Rhoton, P.A., in Tampa, Florida. Mr. Rhoton graduated from the University of Toledo College of Law and has been a member in good standing with The Florida Bar since his admission to practice in 1995. The exclusive focus of Mr. Rhoton's practice is dedicated to assisting Florida inmates with their criminal appeal/postconviction cases.

Mr. Rhoton is a member of The Florida Bar's Appellate Division. He is also a member of the U.S. District Court, in and for the Middle and Northern Districts of Florida. Mr. Rhoton is licensed to practice before the U.S. Court of Appeals for the 11th Circuit and is also certified to practice before the U.S. Supreme Court. Mr. Rhoton regularly practices before Federal District Courts and the U.S. Court of Appeals for the 11th Circuit.

Mr. Rhoton typically deals with clients who have lengthy prison sentences. Mr. Rhoton has investigated and pursued hundreds of postconviction cases. He has practiced in all phases of the Florida Judicial System, all the way from misdemeanor county courts up to the Florida Supreme Court. Additionally, Mr. Rhoton has been directly responsible for amendments to Florida Rule of Criminal Procedure 3.850 (the main vehicle for most postconviction actions). Mr. Rhoton is appointed by the Florida Supreme Court to the Florida Criminal Rules Steering Committee, Subcommittee on Postconviction Relief, which is focused on rewriting Florida Rule of Criminal Procedure 3.850. Mr. Rhoton works on said subcommittee with judges and other governmental officials in an effort to improve the administration and execution of postconviction proceedings. Mr. Rhoton's role on said committee has been to advocate for changes that will be beneficial to postconviction litigants (inmates).

For over a decade, Mr. Rhoton authored a bimonthly article, *Post Conviction Corner*, for Florida Prison Legal Perspectives. Selected articles from *Post Conviction Corner* have been compiled and printed in a legal self-help book, *Postconviction Relief for the Florida Prisoner*. Mr. Rhoton also served on the Board of Directors of the Florida Prisoner's Legal Aid Organization, Inc.

Ryan J. Sydejko, Esq.

Ryan J. Sydejko is an attorney with the law office of Loren Rhoton, P.A. His practice focuses primarily on postconviction matters for those incarcerated throughout the State of Florida. He has argued cases before many circuit courts and District Courts of Appeal and has several published opinions. Mr. Sydejko has also presented cases to the Supreme Court of Florida and the U.S. District Courts for the Middle and Northern Districts of Florida.

Mr. Sydejko graduated from the University of Minnesota with a degree in political science and attended the University of Tulsa College of Law. As a student, he authored a law review article entitled: "International Influence on Democracy: How Terrorism Exploited a Deteriorating Fourth Amendment." The article, exploring how domestic terrorist threats have reshaped everyday law enforcement procedures, was published in the Spring 2006 edition of the Wayne State University Law School Journal of Law in Society. Mr. Sydejko also wrote articles for the Florida Prison Legal Perspectives. Mr. Sydejko is a member in good standing with the Florida Bar and is qualified to practice in all Florida state courts, as well as the Federal District Courts for the Middle and Northern Districts of Florida.

The Florida Postconviction Journal

Volume 2
Issue 1

a quarterly publication of Loren Rhoton, P.A.

Notable Firm Cases

Dames v. State, 773 So.2d 563 (Fla. 2d DCA 2000) – Improper summary denial of Rule 3.850 Motion reversed & remanded for evidentiary hearing.

Dames v. State, 807 So.2d 756 (Fla. 2d DCA 2002) – First Degree Murder conviction vacated & new trial granted due to ineffective counsel

Battle v. State, 710 So.2d 628 (Fla. 2d DCA 1998) – Improper Habitual Felony Offender Sentence on violation of probation reversed & remanded for resentencing

Mitchell v. State, 734 So.2d 1067 (Fla. 1st DCA 1999) - counsel can render ineffective assistance for failure to argue boarded-up structure is not a 'dwelling' under arson statute

Caban v. State, 9 So.3d 50 (Fla. 5th DCA 2009) – counsel can be ineffective for failing to object to improper impeachment of defense expert witnesses in Shaken Baby Syndrome case

Graff v. State, 846 So.2d 582 (Fla. 2d DCA 2003) – attorney's misadvice as to potential sentence can amount to ineffective assistance of counsel sufficient to justify withdrawal of plea.

Easley v. State, 742 So.2d 463 (Fla. 2d DCA 1999) – counsel can render ineffective assistance for failure to investigate insanity defense.

Campbell v. State, 16 So.3d 316 (Fla. 2d DCA 2009) – Manifest Injustice – summary denial of Rule 3.800 motion to correct illegal sentence reversed & remanded on manifest injustice grounds.

Thompson v. State, 987 So.2d 727 (Fla. 4th DCA 2008) – Reversal of Life Sentences – entitled to de novo resentencing upon correction of improper consecutive life sentences for murder and burglary.

Williams v. State, 777 So.2d 947 (Fla. 2000) – Right to Belated Postconviction Motion – if postconviction counsel fails to timely file Rule 3.850 Motion, defendant has right to file belated appeal.

Parker v. State, 977 So.2d 671 (Fla. 4th DCA 2008) – Sentence reversed & remanded for resentencing due to judicial vindictiveness

Drafting Postconviction Claims: A Lesson in Brevity

As many Journal readers are likely aware, piling as many issues as possible into a postconviction motion is not typically a good strategy. Take for example, Cortes v. State, 2012 WL 933024 (Fla. 4th DCA 2012).

In Cortes, the defendant filed over seventy claims for relief. While Cortes' enthusiasm for research and writing should be commended, his approach to seeking relief is not. First, there is hardly a trial imaginable in which there were over seventy reversible errors committed. Even if Cortes did have a few good claims, they were almost certainly lost in the labyrinth of meritless issues. The Court found the motion abusive and littered with meritless and frivolous claims. As such, the trial court had discretion to strike the unintelligible motion.

The second problem with Cortes' strategy is that Rule 3.850 was recently amended to impose a fifty-page limit on postconviction motions. See Fla. R. Crim. P. 3.850(c). Truth be told, it is fairly rare for a postconviction motion to require more than fifty pages to properly allege and argue grounds for relief. Occasionally there are decades old cases with lengthy procedural histories that may require additional pages, but for the most part, postconviction motions should fall under that page limitation. If you find yourself greatly exceeding that limit, there are a few options. First, Rule 3.850 allows a movant to seek leave of court to file a lengthier motion upon a showing of good cause. Second, the movant should review his claims and edit as much as possible. Often times in legal writing, arguments can become redundant. In order to not lose the reader (i.e. judge), it is critical to keep the issues concise and directly to the point by limiting tangents and flowery language. Such writing takes practice, but can pay large dividends.

By doing so, you gain credibility with the court (who would realize you know what you're doing) and would prevent those claims from being lost in a sea of frivolity. We can all learn from the lesson in Cortes that throwing in every conceivable claim, and then some, provides the court sufficient grounds to deny the motion without ever even reaching the merits.

Credibility: The Case of the Admittedly Dishonest Cop vs. The Sweet Old Grandma

by Ryan Sydejko

In State v. Beauprez, the Volusia County Circuit Court was recently faced with an all-too-common scenario. The facts were mostly undisputed.

Daytona police received an anonymous tip alleging drug activity at the defendant's home. Officers knocked and were greeted by the defendant's elderly mother. One officer claimed their presence was due to a "911 disconnect" and sought permission to enter. The grandmother permitted entry. A pellet gun was discovered in plain view and the grandmother permitted closer inspection. The officers continued to search. Officers testified that they sought, and received, permission to search further. The grandmother testified that no such permission was sought or granted. One officer opened a drawer in a piece of furniture and discovered drugs. Both parties agreed that the search of the drawer was illegal if conducted without consent of the grandmother. They also agreed that no laws were violated when the police lied to gain entry into the home. The crucial issue then, according to the defense, was credibility. The defendant asserted that the officer diminished his own credibility by admitting to being a liar (to gain entry). Notably, there was no impeachment of the grandmother.

In a fantastically well-written order, the Circuit Court granted the defense motion to suppress the evidence. Judge Will wrote that it may surprise many Americans that police may, without legal ramifications, arrive at one's front door step, without probable cause, and tell an outrageous lie to gain entry. Further astonishing many is the fact that "the state is free to use the bounty of the intrusion to prosecute the homeowner and her guests for crimes discovered in the course of this journey into the heretofore private sanctum of the home." This procedure has evolved into a "knock and talk". The Court noted that this procedure has been very effective in arresting criminals, but noted that perhaps our society ought to aspire to loftier goals than mere expediency.

Dishonesty, as Judge Will wrote, is seldom without consequences for any person. Costs are significant when we teach young officers to lie to citizens, and when we teach citizens that officers are liars. Is honesty a virtue for families and individuals, but only optional for law enforcement? We, as a nation, are better than that. But, as the Court held, the law is the law.

Ultimately, this case was reduced to a credibility stand-off. Most often, the word of the officer is in conflict with the word of the defendant. Integral to our system of jurisprudence is the fact that one's propensity for truth is at least somewhat discernible "by examining his brushes with truth and dishonesty in the past." A liar cannot be trusted.

Judge Will found the State prevailed on the grounds that officers may lie to gain entry to homes. But, more importantly, the State did not prevail on credibility. Just as will all of us, police experience consequences when relying upon dishonest police conduct. Once character is damaged, it is difficult to reconstruct. As Judge Will wrote: "a little boy may falsely call 'wolf' only so many times before no one listens. A liar, after all, is a liar."

New Prisoner Newsletter

In keeping with our efforts to inform prisoners about helpful services, the Florida Postconviction Journal is pleased to introduce The Florida Postconviction Legal Aid Organization, Inc. (FPLAO). FPLAO is now publishing a newsletter for inmates called the Florida Postconviction Legal Perspectives (FPLP). The FPLP addresses issues that are of interest to Florida prisoners such as promoting education and skilled court access for prisoners, as well as promoting accountability of corrections officials. To become a member and receive the monthly FPLP newsletter, contact FPLAO at: 5189 Stewart Street, Milton, Florida 32570. They can also be reached at: (850)454-7095; myfplp@aol.com; and, myfplp.org. Subscriptions cost $18.00 for prisoners, and, $26.00 for family members/individuals. [**The Florida Postconviction Journal is not affiliated with FPLAO or the FPLP, and derives no funds from the subscription costs. We merely provide this information as a service to our readers. DO NOT SEND MONEY TO THE FLORIDA POSTCONVICTION JOURNAL FOR FPLAO MEMBERSHIP. ANY INQUIRIES ABOUT FPLAO MEMBERSHIP MUST BE ADDRESSED TO FPLAO'S ABOVE-LISTED ADDRESS**).

Potential Sentence After Retrial In Capital Cases

by Ryan J. Sydejko

In D'Arcangelo v. State, 2012 WL 879283 (Fla. 2d DCA 2012), the Court was faced with the issue of whether a defendant, who was sentenced to life imprisonment on a first degree murder conviction, would be subject to capital punishment should he succeed on a motion for postconviction relief.

D'Arcangelo was convicted of first degree murder, but the jury split evenly on the issue regarding punishment. The trial court imposed a sentence of life imprisonment. Decades later, D'Arcangelo moved for postconviction relief based upon newly discovered evidence. After that filing, it was determined that D'Arcangelo may have been incompetent. The issue then became whether the death penalty was a potential sentence upon retrial. The reason being that a potentially incompetent D'Arcangelo would be seeking a new trial and subjecting himself to a death sentence, something a competent D'Arcangelo may not have elected to chance.

After proceedings in both the circuit court and District Court of Appeal, the State finally conceded that death was not possible upon retrial. The DCA agreed. The life sentence originally imposed operated as an acquittal of the facts that would have warranted a death sentence.

The Second District Court of Appeal held that a "penalty-phase proceeding in Florida is akin to a trial in which the State must prove its case for the death penalty, first to the jury and then to the trial court. The imposition of a life sentence following penalty proceedings is a determination that the State did not prove its case, and it is therefore an acquittal of the circumstances that would justify the death penalty." Because a potentially incompetent D'Arcangelo was no longer subjecting himself to a more severe sentence, counsel was permitted to proceed on his behalf.

Support Services for Inmates & Their Families Available

If you have a suggestion for a group or inmate resource that should be listed in our newsletter, please contact us with the information and we will share any helpful information in future issues.

Innocence Project of Florida.
1100 East Park Ave.
Tallahassee, FL, 32301
Phone: (850) 561-6767
Assists inmates with postconviction DNA innocence cases and helps exonerees in obtaining compensation for wrongful convictions.

R.I.S.E. (Relations of Inmates Supporting Each-Other).
23184 Allen Avenue,
Port Charlotte, FL, 33980
Phone: (941)421-6907
Contact: Candy Kendrick
Email: RISEFLORIDA@Yahoo.com
Offers support to the friends and families of Florida inmates. Programs include a carpool connection, Books for Inmates, a Christmas toy drive for children of inmates, assistance to out-of-state families visiting Florida inmates, new visitor seminars, and a newsletter.

Florida Legal Services. www.floridalegalhelp.org
2121 Delta Blvd.,   Tallahassee, F
Phone: (904) 385-7900
Provides referrals in civil matters.

Prisontalk.com. An Internet community/forum that provides general information and networking for families of inmates. Also, has Florida specific forum that addresses issues ranging from dealing with the D.O.C. to coping with incarceration.

Florida Justice Institute, Inc.
4320 Bank of America Tower
100 S.E. Second Street
Miami, FL, 33131
Phone: (305) 358-2081
Contact: Randall C. Berg, Jr.
Email: rcberg@floridajusticeinstitute.org
Handles civil-rights cases regarding conditions in prisons and jails; advocates and lobbies on behalf of prisoners.

To Subscribe or Change Your Mailing Address to *The Florida Postconviction Journal:*

The *Florida Postconviction Journal* is currently being provided, free of charge, to Florida inmates who are interested in receiving the helpful advice and information contained in the newsletter. If you wish to have your name added to the newsletter's mailing list, please fill out the form below and mail it to Loren Rhoton, P.A., 412 East Madison Street, Suite 1111, Tampa, FL 33062. For non-inmates interested in subscribing to the newsletter, please forward a money order in the amount of $25 for a one-year subscription.

Please Check One:

☐ New Subscriber

☐ Change of Address

Name _____ DC# _____

Institution Name and Street Address _____

City _____ State _____ Zip _____

Technical Pleading Error or Violation of Due Process?

In <u>Figueroa v. State</u>, 2012 WL 1058893 (Fla. 2d DCA 2012), the defendant was charged with an offense entitled "Robbery with a firearm, F.S. 812.13, 775.087, 777.011, punishable by life felony." The body of the charging document set forth the facts, but failed to allege that Figueroa used a firearm during commission of the robbery. In other words, the title charged robbery with a firearm, while the body of the document charged mere robbery. Figueroa was convicted of robbery with a firearm and was sentenced as a habitual violent felony offender to life with a fifteen year minimum mandatory.

Figueroa raised, numerous times, the illegality of his sentence. In fact, he raised the claim so many times that the circuit court imposed sanctions for frivolous filings. On this final attempt, however, the District Court finally listened.

The Court began by recognizing that when a discrepancy between the heading and body of an charging document exists, the offense described within the body is the one in which the defendant is actually charged. After a thorough analysis, the Court found that the charging document in this case omitted an essential element of the offense; i.e. use of the firearm. That point is crucial, as it distinguishes Figueroa from other cases in which use of a weapon is not an element of the offense, but rather an enhancement.

Case law is clear that "a conviction on a charge not made by the indictment or information is a denial of due process." <u>State v. Gray</u>, 435 So.2d 816, 818 (Fla. 1983). Such a defect "can be raised at any time—before trial, after trial, on appeal, or by habeas corpus." <u>Id.</u> Despite these constitutional implications, the Court found that Figueroa was benefitting from "a rather technical pleading error."

Whether a simple "pleading error" or a violation of Figueroa's fundamental right to due process of law, the Court recognized that this case presented the "'uncommon and extraordinary circumstances' constituting manifest injustice." Thus, postconviction relief was due.

Figueroa's life sentence as a habitual violent felony offender with a minimum mandatory of fifteen years for armed robbery was reduced to no more than thirty years incarceration, with a minimum mandatory of ten years for simple robbery.

For the postconviction movant, review of the Figueroa opinion can be helpful as the Court provides a rather detailed analysis of when a charging document deficiency relates to the actual offense, or merely an enhancement. That distinction is critical when considering whether one's sentence merits postconviction review.

The Florida Postconviction Journal

Volume 2
Issue 1

a quarterly publication of Loren Rhoton, P.A.

Mitigated Sentences and Requirement Defendant Demonstrate DOC's Inability to Render Care

In State v. Chubbick, 37 Fla. L. Weekly D582 (Fla. 4th DCA 2012), the Fourth DCA re-examined the requirement that a defendant demonstrate DOC's inability to render proper care in a motion to mitigate sentence based upon disability or illness. Florida appellate courts have uniformly held that in order to receive a sentence below the guidelines, the defense must show: (1) the defendant suffers from a mental or physical disorder; (2) he is amenable to treatment; and (3) such treatment is not available in DOC.

The controlling statute here is Fla. Stat. §921.0026(2)(d). The Legislature dictated that a sentence below the minimum was permissible if "the defendant requires specialized treatment for a mental disorder that is unrelated to substance abuse or addition or for a physical disability, and the defendant is amenable to treatment." Because the Legislature did not explicitly require a defendant to prove DOC incapable of rendering adequate care, the Fourth DCA reversed a long line of cases and certified conflict with nine others. This additional element, the Fourth DCA found, was added in State v. Abrams, 706 So.2d 903 (Fla. 2d DCA 1998), and subsequently adopted and glossed over by every court since then.

In an earlier opinion, the Fifth DCA acknowledged that "a lack of available treatment in prison is not required under the statute. Although illness is not a 'get out of jail free card', a treatable physical disability is one of the circumstances where the legislature has chosen to re-invest trial judges with discretion to vary from sentencing guidelines." State v. Spioch, 706 So.2d 32, 36 (Fla. 5th DCA 1998).

Despite this early acknowledgment, every Florida court adopted the additional element inserted by Abrams. The difficulty in proving a negative (i.e. that treatment is not available) is very burdensome. The court provided an example where a defense expert had contacted DOC numerous times in order to get an explanation as to DOC's treatment procedures. As commonly happens, DOC officials were not entirely forthcoming. Thus, the defense had to rely on information from other inmates, which likely would be considered hearsay.

This information is important for those postconviction movants who have been recently conviction or whom have been granted a resentencing. While this decision doesn't "open the floodgates" as some have predicted, it does certainly provide the postconviction movant one more viable ground convince a judge that a shorter sentence is proper.

Tips for Choosing Legal Counsel

by Loren D. Rhoton

As reviled as attorneys are (and sometimes for good reason), they do serve an important function in our justice system. A well-trained and experienced lawyer can often make all the difference in the outcome of a case. There is an old adage that a man who has himself for a lawyer has a fool for a client. Clichéd as that saying is, there is a lot of truth in it. I always advise people not to represent themselves in any legal matters if they can avoid it. This especially applies to criminal appeals and postconviction motions. Unfortunately, there is no constitutional right to appointment of postconviction counsel and indigent prisoners usually have to represent their own interests in postconviction proceedings. However, if you are in a position to hire a lawyer for your postconviction case, it is strongly advised that you do so. This article gives some advice on choosing the right attorney in the postconviction setting.

A license to practice law enables an attorney to handle all manners of legal matters both in and out of court. However, the mere possession of a law license does not mean that an attorney is proficient in any given area of the law. Lawyers often focus their practices on a few areas of the law and have little to no practical legal knowledge outside of those areas. For this reason, it is important to make sure that your appellate counsel is experienced with postconviction matters. I have seen too many cases where trial level criminal defense attorneys attempt to handle criminal appeals or postconviction cases and, in the process, end up hopelessly bungling the cases. You want to make sure that you are hiring a competent and experienced postconviction attorney. Don't just hire any lawyer to represent your interests. So, how does one determine that a lawyer is experienced and competent?

There are many ways to learn about an attorney's qualifications. Firstly, one can inquire with the Florida Bar as to whether an attorney has ever been disciplined for misconduct. Any attorney who has practiced for any number of years will likely have had at least one bar complaint filed against him or her. The important inquiry is not if a bar complaint has ever been filed, but, whether the attorney has ever been disciplined. If the attorney has been disciplined, the actions of the Florida Bar will be public record and anybody can obtain a copy of the order imposing discipline on the attorney. If an attorney has repeated violations for failing to represent clients' interests or failure to communicate with clients, these are big red

flags that the attorney's representation may be substandard. It is always acceptable to ask a prospective attorney about whether he or she has ever received any disciplinary action.

It is also important to ask the prospective attorney about his experience with postconviction cases. Ask how long the attorney has been in practice. Ask how many postconviction actions the attorney has handled. Ask how many postconviction evidentiary hearings the attorney has conducted. These questions will give some idea as to whether the attorney has any experience with postconviction cases.

If an attorney guarantees an outcome or says that you will likely win your case, be very careful about hiring such an attorney. The fact of the matter is that postconviction cases are very difficult to win and the majority of such cases are not successful. This is the unfortunate truth about postconviction cases. Therefore, if an attorney gives the indication that you will probably win on your case, it means one of two things: (1) he is lying to you in order get you to hire him; or, (2) he is inexperienced with such cases and has unrealistic expectations. Either way, such an attorney should be avoided. When I discuss a case's potential with a client, the most I can do is explain that the client has a viable postconviction claim and that there is the possibility of prevailing on the claim. Any attorney that goes beyond that is creating unrealistic expectations and giving false hope.

Have your family members speak with the attorney. See what kind of vibe they get from him. Does the lawyer present himself professionally? Does he have a physical office or does he work out of his home and use a P.O. Box for correspondence? This can be a red flag. When an attorney does not have a physical office, he or she can be more difficult to reach. A physical office in the same location over a period of time is one indicator of the a stability of the practice. And it is desirable to have such stability in the professional that is going to be handling your case for perhaps years to come.

Does the attorney answer your initial correspondence? Does he answer your questions to

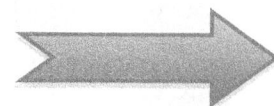

The Florida Postconviction Journal

Volume 2
Issue 1

a quarterly publication of Loren Rhoton, P.A.

Tips for Choosing Legal Counsel (continued)

your satisfaction? Or, does the attorney disregard your comments, suggestions and questions? Does he return your family members' phone calls? Is the attorney available for conferences when requested? These types of things at the beginning of the attorney/client relationship are potential indicators of how you will be treated as your case goes along. If the attorney is not responsive to your questions at the beginning of your case, such treatment will probably continue or worsen as your case goes on.

Finally, ask the prospective attorney for a copy of his written qualifications. This is a good indicator of the attorney's focus. Does he list a great deal of experience with family law or some other unrelated field? Or, do the written qualifications show that the attorney handles mostly postconviction cases? If the qualifications merely show a general practice with no specific area of focus, then the attorney may not be the ideal counsel for a postconviction action.

All of the above suggestions are meant to be helpful in the selection of a postconviction attorney. One final thing to keep in mind is that the client needs to trust his instincts in selecting the attorney. Does something about the things the attorney says make you feel uncomfortable? Or, does the attorney seem to be listening to your concerns and giving you straight answers to your questions? Follow your gut in this regard. I have heard too many people complain about their prior attorneys. They say that they just didn't trust the lawyer from the start, and, that such distrust was later confirmed. Take all of the above considerations into account and then go with the attorney that your instincts tell you is the right one. While all of this does not guarantee that you will hire the perfect lawyer, it certainly will increase the likelihood of satisfaction with the counsel that you choose.

Continuances: When Enough is Enough

Changing lawyers four times just before trial isn't always an advisable strategy. In Ramos v. State, 75 So.3d 1277 (Fla. 4th DCA 2011), the defendant's repeated attorney hiring of new attorneys had disrupted the trial court's calendar as the case had been set for trial five times. Id. at 1279. On the final calendar call, a Thursday, defense counsel, who was hired two to three months prior, stated that he was not ready for trial as additional time was needed to procure deposition transcripts taken by previous counsel. Id. The State had no objection. Id.

The trial court was displeased with the fact that Ramos had been awaiting trial for approximately a year and a half already, and denied a continuance, leaving the jury trial set for Monday. Id.

On Monday, the day of jury trial, defense counsel stated that he had obtained two of the transcripts, but two others were still needed, most notably the deposition of the victim. Id. Jury selection was then conducted, lasting until 8 p.m. Id. Because of the late hour, counsel was unable to pick up the remaining transcripts. Id. After opening statements the following day, the State located a copy of the victim's deposition. Id. While the State examined the victim, copies were made of the deposition. Id. Moments before cross-examination, defense counsel was provided a copy of the deposition. Id. A twenty minute recess was then taken so defense counsel could "breeze through" the deposition. Id. at 1280.

The District Court found that Ramos' own actions were to blame for the predicament. The Court found that Ramos contributed significantly to the lack of preparation time for his counsel since Ramos changed attorneys four times. Id. There was no evidence that any previous attorney had provided ineffective assistance, thus the predicament was of Ramos' own creation. Id. While defense counsel was hired two to three months before trial, he chose to wait until six weeks before trial to complain about a delay in obtaining transcripts. Id. This delayed action by counsel piled on Ramos' delays, further aggravating the situation.

The Court ultimately found that Ramos "reached the point where his right to adequate time for preparation for trial is counterbalanced by the right to the effective administration of justice." Id. at 1281. "His own actions and those of his private counsel of choice were responsible for the lack of adequate preparation time, if any." Id. While many judges are lenient to newly obtained counsel, there does come a time when a timely trial outweighs more defense delays. Understanding where that threshold exists is relevant both to trial strategy and to preparing viable postconviction issues.

Loren Rhoton, P.A.

Postconviction Attorneys

412 East Madison Street
Suite 1111
Tampa, Florida 33602
Tel: 813-226-3138
Fax: 813-221-2182
Email:
lorenrhoton@rhotonpostconviction.com
rsydejko@rhotonpostconviction.com

- Direct Appeals
- Belated Appeals
- Rule 3.850 Motions
- Illegal Sentence Corrections
- Rule 9.141 Petitions
- Federal Habeas Corpus Petitions
- Clemency Petitions and Waivers

The Florida Postconviction Journal publishes up to four times per year. This Journal provides resources for information affecting prisoners, their families, friends, loved ones, and the general public of the State of Florida. Promoting skilled access to the court system for indigent prisoners is a primary goal of this publication. Due to the volume of mail that is received, not all correspondence can be returned. If you would like return of materials, please enclose a postage-paid and pre-addressed envelope. This publication is not meant to be a substitute for legal or other professional advice. The material addressed in the Journal should not be relied upon as authoritative and may not contain sufficient information to deal with specific legal issues.

The Florida Postconviction Journal
a publication of Loren Rhoton, P.A.
412 East Madison Street
Suite 1111
Tampa, FL 33602

CHANGE SERVICE REQUESTED

Name
Institution
Street Address
City, State, Zip

The Florida Postconviction Journal

Volume 2
Issue 2

a quarterly publication of Loren Rhoton, P.A.

Fall 2012

Florida Supreme Court Finds Trafficking Statute Constitutional

In a move that disappoints many, the Florida Supreme Court has held that §893.13, which criminalizes the possession of various drugs, is constitutional and does not violate due process. Previously, the United States District Court for the Middle District of Florida held, in Shelton v. Florida, 802 F.Supp.2d 1289 (2011), that the trafficking/possession statute amounted to a strict liability crime because it eliminated *mens rea* (guilty knowledge) as an element of drug distribution offenses. However, in reviewing a constitutional challenge to §893.13, the Florida Supreme Court found that the statute did not punish essentially innocent conduct, there was no constitutional right to possess controlled substances or to be ignorant of the nature of the property in one's possession, and any concern about punishing innocent conduct was obviated by allowing a defendant to raise affirmative defense of an absence of knowledge. State v. Adkins, --- So.3d ----, 37 F.L.W. S449, (Fla.2012). Thus, Adkins upheld the constitutionality of §893.13.

Also, on the heels of the Adkins decision, the 11th Circuit Court of Appeals reversed the Middle District's ruling in Shelton. Shelton v. Secretary, DOC, 23 Fla. L. Weekly Fed. C 1469 (11th Cir. 2012). Although the reversal in Shelton never actually ruled upon the due process question, the effect is, for the time being, to shut down collateral claims based upon Shelton v. Florida, 802 F.Supp.2d 1289 (2011).

It is currently unclear if Shelton or Adkins will be further pursued in the federal courts. We will keep an eye on the issue with hopes that the unconstitutionality of §893.13 will be adequately addressed. In news in this regard will be published in future issues of *FPJ*. In the meantime, people with convictions under §893.13 would be wise to continue collaterally attacking their convictions based upon the rationale of Shelton v. Florida, 802 F.Supp.2d 1289 (2011), with the hopes that either the 11th Circuit or the United States Supreme Court will address the issue head on.

Loren D. Rhoton

Burglary with Assault Qualifies for PRR Sentencing

In Hackley v. State, 95 So.3d 92 (Fla. 2012), the Florida Supreme Court recently settled inter-district conflict over the question of whether Burglary with Assault is a qualifying offense for Prison Releasee Reoffender sentencing. It was held that Burglary with Battery is not a qualifying PRR offense because it is not an enumerated offense under the statute and does not come under the catchall category that includes "[a]ny felony that involves the use or threat of physical force or violence against an individual."

On the other hand, since an assault necessarily requires "threat by word or act to do violence to the person of another," Burglary with Assault does come under the catchall category and, thus, does qualify for PRR treatment.

Court Errs in Refusing Read-Back of Testimony

In Johnson v. State, 37 Fla. L. Weekly D2217 (Fla. 5th DCA 2012), during jury deliberations, a note was sent to the judge seeking a read-back of trial testimony. The trial court refused, telling the jury: "I don't do [read-backs]" and instead instructed the jury "to rely upon their collective memories of the testimony." Defense counsel objected, but was overruled.

The District Court reversed the conviction, holding that while a trial court has great discretion in determining whether to grant a read-back request, it cannot mislead the jury into believing read-backs are prohibited. See Hazuri v. State, 91 So.2d 836 (Fla. 2012). As a result, Johnson was granted a new trial. For an extensive discussion regarding how requests for read-backs should be handled, see the Florida Supreme Court's opinion in Hazuri.

The Florida Postconviction Journal

page 2 of 10 a quarterly publication of Loren Rhoton, P.A.

<u>About Loren Rhoton, P.A.</u>

Loren Rhoton, P.A. is a law firm that focuses exclusively on postconviction actions and inmate issues. The mission of Loren Rhoton, P.A. is to ensure that justice is accomplished in each and every case the firm undertakes. The firm's area of practice ranges from direct criminal appeals and postconviction actions to assisting inmates in dealing with the Florida Department of Corrections. Loren Rhoton, P.A., is a small firm, consisting of Mr. Loren D. Rhoton and Mr. Ryan J. Sydejko. The firm strives to keep a small caseload in order to give each case the individual attention it deserves. We are not a volume business. We do not accept every case that is presented to the firm for representation. A thorough review of any potential case will be conducted before the firm undertakes full representation. If you wish to have your case reviewed for representation, please contact Loren Rhoton for more information. If inquiring about representation, please do not send any materials to the firm that you wish to have returned to you.

Loren D. Rhoton, Esq.

Loren D. Rhoton is an attorney in private practice with the law office of Loren Rhoton, P.A., in Tampa, Florida. Mr. Rhoton graduated from the University of Toledo College of Law and has been a member in good standing with The Florida Bar since his admission to practice in 1995. The exclusive focus of Mr. Rhoton's practice is dedicated to assisting Florida inmates with their criminal appeal/postconviction cases.

Mr. Rhoton is a member of The Florida Bar's Appellate Division. He is also a member of the U.S. District Court, in and for the Middle and Northern Districts of Florida. Mr. Rhoton is licensed to practice before the U.S. Court of Appeals for the 11th Circuit and is also certified to practice before the U.S. Supreme Court. Mr. Rhoton regularly practices before Federal District Courts and the U.S. Court of Appeals for the 11th Circuit.

Mr. Rhoton typically deals with clients who have lengthy prison sentences. Mr. Rhoton has investigated and pursued hundreds of postconviction cases. He has practiced in all phases of the Florida Judicial System, all the way from misdemeanor county courts up to the Florida Supreme Court. Additionally, Mr. Rhoton has been directly responsible for amendments to Florida Rule of Criminal Procedure 3.850 (the main vehicle for most postconviction actions). Mr. Rhoton is appointed by the Florida Supreme Court to the Florida Criminal Rules Steering Committee, Subcommittee on Postconviction Relief, which is focused on rewriting Florida Rule of Criminal Procedure 3.850. Mr. Rhoton works on said subcommittee with judges and other governmental officials in an effort to improve the administration and execution of postconviction proceedings. Mr. Rhoton's role on said committee has been to advocate for changes that will be beneficial to postconviction litigants (inmates).

For over a decade, Mr. Rhoton authored a bimonthly article, *Post Conviction Corner*, for Florida Prison Legal Perspectives. Selected articles from *Post Conviction Corner* have been compiled and printed in a legal self-help book, *Postconviction Relief for the Florida Prisoner*. Mr. Rhoton also served on the Board of Directors of the Florida Prisoner's Legal Aid Organization, Inc.

Ryan J. Sydejko, Esq.

Ryan J. Sydejko is an attorney with the law office of Loren Rhoton, P.A. His practice focuses primarily on postconviction matters for those incarcerated throughout the State of Florida. He has argued cases before many circuit courts and District Courts of Appeal and has several published opinions. Mr. Sydejko has also presented cases to the Supreme Court of Florida and the U.S. District Courts for the Middle and Northern Districts of Florida.

Mr. Sydejko graduated from the University of Minnesota with a degree in political science and attended the University of Tulsa College of Law. As a student, he authored a law review article entitled: "International Influence on Democracy: How Terrorism Exploited a Deteriorating Fourth Amendment." The article, exploring how domestic terrorist threats have reshaped everyday law enforcement procedures, was published in the Spring 2006 edition of the Wayne State University Law School Journal of Law in Society. Mr. Sydejko also wrote articles for the Florida Prison Legal Perspectives. Mr. Sydejko is a member in good standing with the Florida Bar and is qualified to practice in all Florida state courts, as well as the Federal District Courts for the Middle and Northern Districts of Florida.

The Florida Postconviction Journal

Volume 2
Issue 2

a quarterly publication of Loren Rhoton, P.A.   page 3 of 10

Notable Firm Cases

Dames v. State, 773 So.2d 563 (Fla. 2d DCA 2000) – Improper summary denial of Rule 3.850 Motion reversed & remanded for evidentiary hearing.

Dames v. State, 807 So.2d 756 (Fla. 2d DCA 2002) – First Degree Murder conviction vacated & new trial granted due to ineffective counsel

Battle v. State, 710 So.2d 628 (Fla. 2d DCA 1998) – Improper Habitual Felony Offender Sentence on violation of probation reversed & remanded for resentencing

Mitchell v. State, 734 So.2d 1067 (Fla. 1st DCA 1999) - counsel can render ineffective assistance for failure to argue boarded-up structure is not a 'dwelling' under arson statute

Caban v. State, 9 So.3d 50 (Fla. 5th DCA 2009) – counsel can be ineffective for failing to object to improper impeachment of defense expert witnesses in Shaken Baby Syndrome case

Graff v. State, 846 So.2d 582 (Fla. 2d DCA 2003) – attorney's misadvice as to potential sentence can amount to ineffective assistance of counsel sufficient to justify withdrawal of plea.

Easley v. State, 742 So.2d 463 (Fla. 2d DCA 1999) – counsel can render ineffective assistance for failure to investigate insanity defense.

Campbell v. State, 16 So.3d 316 (Fla. 2d DCA 2009) – Manifest Injustice – summary denial of Rule 3.800 motion to correct illegal sentence reversed & remanded on manifest injustice grounds.

Thompson v. State, 987 So.2d 727 (Fla. 4th DCA 2008) – Reversal of Life Sentences – entitled to *de novo* resentencing upon correction of improper consecutive life sentences for murder and burglary.

Williams v. State, 777 So.2d 947 (Fla. 2000) – Right to Belated Postconviction Motion – if post-conviction counsel fails to timely file Rule 3.850 Motion, defendant has right to file belated appeal.

Parker v. State, 977 So.2d 671 (Fla. 4th DCA 2008) – Sentence reversed & remanded for resentencing due to judicial vindictiveness.

Biomechanics Experts & Shaken Baby Syndrome

In Council v. State, Fla. L. Weekly D1721 (Fla. 1st DCA 2012), Council was found guilty of aggravated child abuse. At trial, the State alleged that the victim suffered from Shaken Baby Syndrome and introduced expert medical testimony in support of that position.

Council, in order to combat such testimony, retained his own doctor, an expert in biomechanics. The trial court did not permit the defense's expert who would have testified that the victim's injuries could have been caused by an accidental fall from a day bed. The trial court reasoned that the defense expert's testimony would have confused the jury because such testimony in the field of biomechanics could not translate into a medical diagnosis regarding the extent of the victim's injury.

The trial court was correct in one regard: that a biomechanics expert is not qualified to give a medical opinion regarding the extent of an injury. Stockwell v. Drake, 901 So.2d 974, 976 (Fla. 4th DCA 2005). But, the defense expert in Council was not offering an opinion as to the extent of the injury, but rather an opinion that the victim's injuries could have been caused by an accidental fall from a daybed and that shaking alone could not have cause such injuries. The District Court found that such opinions went to causation based upon the mechanism of injury and therefore fell within the field of biomechanics.

The District Court also found that the error was not harmless. Although the defense did present other expert testimony at trial, that expert had not conducted studies on brain injuries resulting from short falls; nor was he allowed to testify that the victim's injuries could not have been caused by shaking. It was therefore determined that the trial court abused its discretion in excluding the defense expert's testimony which was relevant and would have assisted the jury in resolving a highly contested factual issue (there was no eyewitness testimony nor any direct evidence of intentional abuse). As a result, the District Court reversed and remanded for a new trial.

The Florida Postconviction Journal

page 4 of 10   a quarterly publication of Loren Rhoton, P.A.

Claims of Newly Discovered Evidence & Confusion as to the Applicable Standard

by Ryan Sydejko

It is not uncommon for the criminally accused to locate evidence which was not available at the time of their trial. Such evidence can take many forms, from physical evidence to eyewitness testimony, to recanted trial testimony. Some even involve business records or government documents not previously available. The method most frequently used to challenge's ones conviction after such findings is a claim of newly discovered evidence pursuant to Rule 3.850.

The Rules set forth the pleading requirements: the evidence is new and could not have been discovered with due diligence before trial, the new evidence is material, and would have probably changed the verdict. Fla. R. Crim. P. 3.600(a)(3). The standard for granting a new trial based upon newly discovered evidence is the same under Fla. R. Crim. P. 3.600(a)(3) as the postconviction claim under Fla. R. Crim. P. 3.850(b)(1). Totta v. State, 740 So.2d 57, 58 (Fla. 4th DCA 1999).

Once those elements are alleged in a pleading, there appears to be confusion amongst some courts as to what standard of review to apply. The objective of this article is to review the proper standard so potential postconviction movants know ahead of time what a trial court may do.

After the motion is filed, the postconviction court has two findings to make: (1) whether the motion is facially sufficient; and (2) whether an evidentiary hearing is warranted. Nordelo v. State, 93 So.3d 178, 185 (Fla. 2012). The distinction between these two is important and often confused by State Attorneys responding to the claims and by the postconviction courts when summarily denying the claims.

For instance, in Nordelo, the defendant filed a postconviction newly discovered evidence claim, asserting that a co-defendant had new testimony of exculpatory nature. Id. at 180. The postconviction court held a hearing to determine whether an evidentiary hearing was required. Id. at 181. After this preliminary hearing, the court concluded that the evidence did not qualify as newly discovered as it could have been obtained earlier through the exercise of due diligence, and therefore summarily denied the claim. Id. The appellate court affirmed, additionally holding that Nordelo's claim was conclusively refuted by the record as the State presented overwhelming evidence of guilt during trial. Id. at 182.

In dissent, Judge Cope wrote that the trial and appellate courts commingled the two separate preliminary findings. Nordelo v. State, 47 So.3d, 854 856-858 (Fla. 3d DCA 2010). Judge Cope observed the distinction between the requirements to (a) plead the existence of newly discovered evidence; and (b) the heightened requirement to establish due diligence during an evidentiary hearing. Id. "The pleading requirement is lower; the proof requirement is higher." Id. The Florida Supreme Court has encountered similar confusion, and wrote the following explanation:

The postconviction trial court appears to have *incorrectly applied the heightened requirements to establish due diligence during an evidentiary hearing to evaluate the allegations at a pleading stage.* However, permitting a newly discovered evidence claim to proceed to an evidentiary hearing does *not* establish that the recanted testimony qualifies as newly discovered evidence as a matter of law. (citation omitted) The newly discovered evidence claim remains to be factually tested in an evidentiary hearing to determine whether the defendant has demonstrated that the successive motion has been filed within the time limit for when the statement was or could have been discovered through the exercise of due diligence. (citation omitted) The motion here was sufficiently pled to allow the opportunity to prove through the testimony of witnesses that the threshold requirement of due diligence was satisfied. Accordingly, the postconviction trial court erred in summarily denying this claim on the basis that the pleading failed to sufficiently satisfy the due diligence requirement at that stage of the proceeding. Davis v. State, 26 So.3d 519, 526 (Fla. 2009) (emphasis in original).

In Nordelo, the court reversed the decision, finding the same confusion. Remember, the postconviction court has two preliminary decisions to make: (1) whether the motion is facially sufficient; and (2) whether an evidentiary hearing is warranted. It is not proper for the court to delve into due diligence without providing the opportunity to prove that element in an evidentiary hearing. The standard to get a hearing is lower, the standard to succeed in gaining relief is much higher. Nordelo, 47 So.3d, at 856-858. Keep these differing standards in mind when pleading the claim, and also should a motion for rehearing become necessary.

When Judges and Prosecutors are "Friends"

by Ryan J. Sydejko

In <u>Domville v. State</u>, 2012 WL 3826764 (Fla. 4th DCA, September 5, 2012), the court was faced with a situation where the lower court judge and prosecutor were Facebook friends.

Domville had filed a motion to disqualify the trial judge based upon a fear the judge could not be fair and impartial given the judge's friendship with the prosecutor and attributed adverse rulings to that relationship. The lower court denied the motion as legally insufficient.

The appellate court began by noting that a motion for disqualification is legally sufficient if "the facts alleged (which must be taken as true) would prompt a reasonably prudent person to fear that he could not get a fair and impartial trial." <u>Domville</u>, citing <u>Brofman v. Fla. Hearing Care Ctr., Inc.</u>, 703 So.2d 1191, 1192 (Fla. 4th DCA 1997). The movant needn't prove an actual bias, but instead merely that an objectively reasonable person in a similar situation would also fear a lack of impartiality.

The court turned to a Judicial Ethics Advisory Committee opinion for guidance. JEAC Op. 2009-20 (Nov. 17, 2009). The Committee concluded that the Florida Code of Judicial Conduct precludes a judge from becoming "friends" on social networking sites with lawyers appearing before that judge. The danger is that a public acknowledgment of that friendship could convey to others the impression that the lawyer is in a special position to influence the judge. <u>Domville</u>, citing Fla. Code Jud. Conduct Canon 2B.

Because Domville had "alleged facts that would create in a reasonably prudent person a well-founded fear of not receiving a fair and impartial trial", the court quashed the order denying disqualification and remanded.

Support Services for Inmates & Their Families Available

If you have a suggestion for a group or inmate resource that should be listed in our newsletter, please contact us with the information and we will share any helpful information in future issues.

The Florida Postconviction Legal Aid Organization, Inc. – www.myfplp.org
P.O. Box 4104, Milton, FL 32572
Phone: (850) 400-1205; Email: myfplp@aol.com
***FPLAO publishes a newsletter for inmates called the Florida Postconviction Legal Perspectives (FPLP). The FPLP addresses issues of interest to Florida prisoners such as promoting accountability of corrections officials. To become a member and receive monthly FPLP newsletters, contact FPLAO as the address above. Subscriptions cost $18.00 for prisoners and $26.00 for family members/individuals. [The Florida Postconviction Journal is not affiliated with FPLAO or FPLP, and derives no funds from the subscription costs. We merely provide this information as a service to our readers. DO NOT SEND MONEY TO THE FLORIDA POSTCONVICTION JOURNAL FOR FPLAO MEMBERSHIP. ALL INQUIRIES ABOUT FPLAO MEMBERSHIP MUST BE ADDRESSED TO FPLAO'S ADDRESS ABOVE.

Florida Legal Services, Inc.
www.floridalegalhelp.org
2425 Torreya Dr.,☐Tallahassee, FL, 32303
Phone: (850) 385-7900; Fax: (850) 385-9998
  *Provides referrals in civil matters.

Prisontalk.com.   An Internet community/forum that provides general information and networking for families of inmates. Also, has Florida specific forum that addresses issues ranging from dealing with the D.O.C. to coping with incarceration.

Florida Justice Institute, Inc.
4320 Bank of America Tower☐
100 S.E. Second Street☐
Miami, FL, 33131
Phone: (305) 358-2081
Contact: Randall C. Berg, Jr.
Email: rcberg@floridajusticeinstitute.org
  *Handles civil-rights cases regarding conditions in prisons and jails; advocates and lobbies on behalf of prisoners.

Innocence Project of Florida.
1100 East Park Ave.
Tallahassee, FL, 32301☐
Phone: (850) 561-6767
  *Assists inmates with postconviction DNA innocence cases and helps exonerees in obtaining compensation for wrongful convictions.

To Subscribe or Change Your Mailing Address
to *The Florida Postconviction Journal:*

The *Florida Postconviction Journal* is currently being provided, free of charge, to Florida inmates who are interested in receiving the helpful advice and information contained in the newsletter. If you wish to have your name added to the newsletter's mailing list, please fill out the form below and mail it to Loren Rhoton, P.A., 412 East Madison Street, Suite 1111, Tampa, FL 33062. For non-inmates interested in subscribing to the newsletter, please forward a money order in the amount of $25 for a one-year subscription.

Please Check One:

☐ New Subscriber

☐ Change of Address

Name   DC#

Institution Name and Street Address

City   State   Zip

Introduction of Unrelated Firearm Constitutes Reversible Error

Metayer v. State, 89 So.3d 1002 (Fla. 4th DCA 2012), involves nearly everything one would expect from a Hollywood script: money, drugs, girl friends that hide money and drugs, rival drug dealers, and a triple shooting.

Victims Operle and Jacobs were friends and had been drinking all night. They returned home around 5:30 a.m. and drank more alcohol and smoked a cigar rolled with marijuana and cocaine. Later that morning, defendant Metayer and co-defendant Young contacted Operle. Operle was friends with Young, as both were known drug dealers.

They all sat down to have breakfast while Young and Jacobs completed a drug deal. Everyone then took out and compared their guns. While the guns were on the table, Young stood up and shot Jacobs in the chest. Operle tried to run, but was shot in the shoulder. Young pointed the gun at Operle's face and pulled the trigger, but the gun jammed. Young then kicked Operle in the face. Operle had a seizure and went temporarily unconscious.

Young told Metayer to finish Jacobs off. Metayer got up, grabbed a gun, stood over Jacobs, and shot him in the face. Jacobs died at the scene. While Operle played dead, Young stook Operle's shoes, wallet and watch.

Meanwhile, victim Hunt was sleeping in the bedroom. Young burst into the room and shot Hunt in the back. Young pulled the trigger again, but the gun jammed. Young then shot Hunt again, just above the hip. Hunt passed out.

Young was arrested the next day, and police recovered guns, drugs and money from Young's girlfriend's house. Metayer was arrested about six months later at his mother's house. Two guns were recovered from Metayer's house.

One of the issues at trial was who shot whom, and with which gun. One of the guns recovered from Young's girlfriend's house matched casings found at the scene. The guns recovered from Metayer's house did not match any casings, but the firearms expert did testify that one of Metayer's guns could have been used, there just wasn't any conclusive evidence.

The District Court held that it was error to admit Metayer's two guns into evidence at trial. In order to admit a gun, there must be a "sufficient link between the weapon and the crime." A gun different from the one used in a crime is not relevant to prove that the crime occurred. Therefore, the error was not harmless as evidence of irrelevant collateral crimes is presumed harmful.

The Florida Postconviction Journal

Volume 2
Issue 2

a quarterly publication of Loren Rhoton, P.A.

Standards Will Differ Depending Upon Statutory Vehicle Used in Pursuit of Postconviction Relief

When pursuing postconviction relief, it is critical to understand the standard of review that applies to each claim. In researching the claims, remember that the same claim may have different standards, depending upon which postconviction vehicle is used; i.e. Florida Rules of Criminal Procedure 3.800 or 3.850.

In Kelsey v. State, 37 Fla. L. Weekly D2242 (Fla. 2d DCA 2012), a *pro se* inmate, Kelsey, had filed a Rule 3.800(a) motion to correct an illegal sentence. Kelsey had alleged a scoresheet error. The circuit court summarily denied relief, finding that even if an error had occurred, the same sentence could have been imposed.

At this point, some explanation is needed: when attempting to fix a scoresheet error under Rule 3.800(a), the court will utilize the "could-have-been-imposed" test. Brooks v. State, 969 So.2d 238 (Fla. 2007). Essentially, if the same sentence could have been imposed with a corrected scoresheet, no relief is due. This is a difficult burden to meet.

If, however, relief is sought pursuant to Rule 3.850, the "would-have-been-imposed" test applies. State v. Anderson, 905 So.2d 111 (Fla. 2005). In that situation, it must be clear that the trial court would have imposed the same sentence, had it had the benefit of reviewing the correct scoresheet. Brooks, 969 So.2d at 241-242.

In Kelsey, the District Court did not appear to take issue with the trial court's ruling that Kelsey's claim failed under the could-have-been-imposed standard. Luckily for Kelsey, though, the motion had been filed within Rule 3.850's two-year period of limitations. Thus, the District Court attempted to treat Kelsey's 3.800 motion as a 3.850 motion. In doing so, the District Court explicitly stated that: "if treated as a motion filed pursuant to rule 3.850, it appears that [Kelsey] would be entitled to relief because the 'would-have-been-imposed' test, rather than the 'could-have-been-imposed' test, would apply." Because Kelsey's 3.800 motion did not meet the statutory requirements for a rule 3.850 motion, the District Court was ultimately unable to treat the motion under rule 3.850. Thus, the case was remanded to the lower court with directions that Kelsey be provided an opportunity to amend the claim in a facially sufficient rule 3.850 motion.

This case provides multiple important lessons for the pro se litigant: know which standard of review applies to the claim, know that the standard may change depending on the vehicle, and ensure the motion meets all of the statutory prerequisites.

Limiting Scope of Evidentiary Hearing Testimony

by Loren D. Rhoton

It has long been a concern of mine that testimony given during a postconviction evidentiary hearing will be used against my client at a retrial. This is because when a 3.850 motion involves questions of attorney ineffectiveness, the movant must waive his attorney-client privilege relating to conversations with the original trial/plea attorney. *See*, Lopez v. Singletery, 634 So.2d 1054 (Fla. 1993). Likewise, if the postconviction movant has to testify to support any claims, there is the possibility that the prosecutor could attempt to exploit the situation to elicit admissions about the case from the defendant, which could then later be used against the defendant at a retrial (if one is granted). Unfortunately, there is no Florida caselaw that adequately addresses this situation. As a result, I have made it my pet issue to get the Florida Courts to address such a situation.

In any postconviction case where an evidentiary hearing is granted, the above concerns will likely arise. Therefore, I advise filing a motion, prior to the evidentiary hearing, asking the court to limit the use of any privileged/protected testimony solely to the 3.850 proceedings. It should be argued that while the testimony of the trial attorney and/or the defendant are clearly relevant to the ineffectiveness of counsel claims under consideration by the court, the applicability of said evidence should be limited solely to the postconviction proceedings. In other words, it would be fundamentally unfair to allow any evidence adduced in the 3.850 proceedings to be later used against the defendant at a new trial (should one be granted). The waiver of the 3.850 movant's attorney-client privilege only occurs because of the claim of ineffectiveness of counsel. Thus, should the court grant the 3.850 motion based upon a finding of ineffectiveness of trial counsel, the defendant should not be punished as a result of his attorney's failures. Instead, the defendant should be placed in the position that he was prior to trial, i.e., that no privileged material should be presented against him.

The waiver of the attorney-client privilege and the right to remain silent should be construed narrowly so as to preclude use of confidential information at a new trial or retrial (should such a trial be granted). In Bittaker v. Woodford, 331 F.3d 715 (9th Cir. 2003), it was held that the scope of a habeas corpus petitioner's waiver arising from claim of ineffective assistance of counsel extended only to litigation of the federal habeas

petition; and, therefore, the attorney-client privilege was not waived for all time and all purposes, including the possible retrial of the petitioner, if he was successful in setting aside his original conviction or sentence. Likewise, addressing the same issue, U.S. v. Pinson, 584 F.3d 972, 978 (10th Cir. 2009) held that a court must impose a waiver no broader than needed to ensure the fairness of the proceedings before it.

Also, in Simmons v. U.S., 390 U.S. 377, 394, 88 S.Ct. 967, 976 (1968), it was noted that where testimony of the defendant was required to support a 4th Amendment suppression claim, an undeniable tension is created between the protection against illegal searches and seizures and the 5th Amendment protection against self-incrimination and, therefore, "when a defendant testifies in support of a motion to suppress evidence on Fourth Amendment grounds, his testimony may not thereafter be admitted against him at trial on the issue of guilt unless he makes no objection." A similar dilemma is created when a postconviction movant must testify at an evidentiary hearing; in order to support the burden of proof about ineffectiveness of a trial attorney attorney, a defendant may have to testify and thus be subjected to questions about his case. If said testimony would later be used against the defendant at a retrial, then a tension is created between the defendant's 5th Amendment right to remain silent and his ability to adequately pursue his 6th Amendment right to effective assistance of counsel. Just as with Simmons, such a dilemma should be remedied by limiting the use of the postconviction movant's testimony to the collateral proceedings and precluding any use of his testimony at a retrial.

The matters addressed in this article present what appears to be a novel but important question of law in Florida. I recommend that the above arguments be raised for any 3.850 evidentiary hearing where the trial attorney and/or defendant will have to testify. It is recommended that a motion be filed in advance of the evidentiary hearing and that a ruling on the motion be requested from the court before any testimony and or evidence is presented at the 3.850 evidentiary hearing.

The Florida Postconviction Journal

Volume 2
Issue 2

a quarterly publication of Loren Rhoton, P.A.

The Importance of Knowing Filing Deadlines & How They Are Properly Calculated

One of the most important things to keep in mind for any person navigating the legal system, whether *pro se* or as a licensed attorney, is filing deadlines. Determining which time frames apply to which motion or order can often times be quite difficult, especially for the incarcerated acting *pro se*. In other instances, the time frame is obvious, but tolling may come into play. This is especially true when calculating the time for filing a Federal Writ of Habeas Corpus.

Tolling, or the lack thereof, can eliminate one's ability to appeal to the District Court of Appeal. *See* Outlaw v. State, 2012 WL 3822128 (Fla. 2d DCA, September 5, 2012).

In Outlaw, an order denying relief was entered against Outlaw. Counsel subsequently filed a motion for rehearing, but it was filed more than fifteen days after entrance of the final order. The lower court did eventually rule on the motion. The problem, however, was that was done after the thirty day period that

Outlaw had to file his notice of appeal to the District Court.

Outlaw subsequently attempted an appeal, but the District Court found that it did not have jurisdiction because the notice of appeal was untimely. Outlaw was not saved by the fact that a motion for rehearing was filed since it was untimely and therefore did not toll the thirty day period. Additionally, the period was not tolled by the fact that the lower court acted upon the untimely motion for rehearing. *See* Reid v. Cooper, 955 So.2d 31, 32 (Fla. 3d DCA 2007) ("holding that an untimely motion for rehearing is a nullity and does not toll the time in which to file an appeal).

In other words, Outlaw missed out on an opportunity to appeal the lower court's decision because of a misunderstanding as to the calculation of a period of limitations. It is absolutely critical that readers of *FPJ* be aware of not only the period of limitations, but also how to properly calculate that period so as not to inadvertently waive valuable appellate opportunities.

Indigent Inmate Appealing 3.800 Denial Entitled to Record on Appeal

As many postconviction movants have realized, it can occasionally be difficult to get a clerk of court to properly prepare the record on appeal. And, in some cases, it may even be difficult to get the clerk of court to prepare the record at all.

In Williams v. State, 2012 WL 4801246 (Fla. 2d DCA 2012), the District Court was faced with a petition from a *pro se* inmate who alleged that the clerk of the lower court refused to prepare the record on appeal. Williams had moved the circuit court for an order directing the clerk to prepare the record, at no cost. But, the circuit court held that while Williams could file the postconviction motion at no cost, Williams was not similarly entitled to preparation of the record at no charge. Thus, the clerk of court demanded payment for the record.

Williams subsequently petitioned the District Court via a writ of mandamus and a writ of prohibition. While these were not the best vehicles, the District Court was able to determine what Williams had intended, and interpreted his petition as addressing the District Court's authority to control preparation of the

record under the Florida Rules of Appellate Procedure.

The Court agreed that Williams was entitled to preparation of the record on appeal, at no cost. To do otherwise, the court reasoned, "would result in an unlawful chilling of a criminal defendant's right to appeal or otherwise challenge the propriety or constitutionality of the conviction or sentence. Id. (quoting Schmidt v. Crusoe, 878 So.2d 361, 367 (Fla. 2003).

Importantly, however, the District Court noted that Williams was not entitled to a free personal copy of the record. Instead, only the official record, sent to the District Court, would come at no cost. Should Williams desire a personal copy, that would requirement payment of the clerk's invoice.

Should a *pro se* inmate ever encounter a clerk refusing to prepare the record, review of Williams could be beneficial at it provides a great roadmap as to how to address the situation, citing the relevant statutes and rules, as well as discussing the proper vehicles for such review.

Loren Rhoton, P.A.

Postconviction Attorneys

412 East Madison Street
Suite 1111
Tampa, Florida 33602
Tel: 813-226-3138
Fax: 813-221-2182
Email:
lorenrhoton@rhotonpostconviction.com
rsydejko@rhotonpostconviction.com

- Direct Appeals
- Belated Appeals
- Rule 3.850 Motions
- Illegal Sentence Corrections
- Rule 9.141 Petitions
- Federal Habeas Corpus Petitions
- Clemency Petitions and Waivers

The Florida Postconviction Journal publishes up to four times per year. This Journal provides resources for information affecting prisoners, their families, friends, loved ones, and the general public of the State of Florida. Promoting skilled access to the court system for indigent prisoners is a primary goal of this publication. Due to the volume of mail that is received, not all correspondence can be returned. If you would like return of materials, please enclose a postage-paid and pre-addressed envelope. This publication is not meant to be a substitute for legal or other professional advice. The material addressed in the Journal should not be relied upon as authoritative and may not contain sufficient information to deal with specific legal issues.

The Florida Postconviction Journal
a publication of Loren Rhoton, P.A.
412 East Madison Street
Suite 1111
Tampa, FL 33602

CHANGE SERVICE REQUESTED

Name
Institution
Street Address
City, State, Zip

The Florida Postconviction Journal

Volume 2
Issue 3

a quarterly publication of Loren Rhoton, P.A.

Spring 2013

Welcome!

Welcome to the first issue of the Florida Postconviction Journal for 2013. The newsletter's readership has grown quite a bit since our first issue. The Office of Loren Rhoton, P.A., continues to provide free copies of FPJ to inmates. The letters of thanks from appreciative readers make it worth the effort to continue printing the FPJ.

We are glad to know that we are providing a much-needed service in helping to educate and empower inmates with the knowledge necessary to seek justice in their cases. If you find the newsletter helpful, please pass it along to others after you have had a chance to read it. Spread the word and let people know that we do provide subscriptions free of charge to Florida prisoners. And as always, we welcome suggestions for articles relating to postconviction issues. Thank you to all of our readers. It is a pleasure and rewarding to be able to provide the FPJ to those who need it the most.

No Stipulation to Factual Basis During Plea

In order for a court to accept a plea, a factual basis must be provided. In Hodges v. State, 107 So.3d 538 (Fla. 2d DCA 2013), the parties stipulated to a factual basis, without ever putting those facts on the record.

In a postconviction motion, Hodges argued that his plea was involuntary because there was no factual basis for his plea. Id. at 539. Furthermore, Hodges alleged that a conviction could not stand because there was no evidence that he committed any of the alleged offenses. Id.

Reviewing the record, the DCA determined that the parties agreed to the information contained within the probable cause affidavits, but failed to make those affidavits part of the record. Id. at 540. As such, there was no record material to refute Hodges' claims, requiring remand with directions to hold an evidentiary hearing. Id.

When Does an Extra Comma Require a New Trial?

The Second DCA recently encountered this question in Talley v. State, 106 So.3d 1015 (Fla. 2d DCA 2013). Talley was charged with aggravated battery and battery. Talley alleged the victim attacked first, and Talley was justified in using nondeadly force in self-defense. The victim, meanwhile, testified that Talley attacked first and the victim struck back in self-defense.

The trial court read the standard jury instruction on self-defense, in relevant part: "[Talley] had the right to stand his ground and meet force with force, including deadly force, if he reasonably believed that it was necessary to do so to prevent death or great bodily harm." Talley was found guilty of the lesser-included offense of felony battery and sentenced to almost six years in prison.

Talley argued on appeal that the standard jury instruction, which includes a comma after "including

deadly force" eliminated his only defense. The Stand Your Ground statute does not include that extra comma; in relevant part: "has the right to stand his or her ground and meet force with force, including deadly force if he or she reasonably believes it is necessary to do so to prevent death or great bodily harm." Fla. Stat. 776.013 (2012).

The DCA agreed with Talley, holding that the extra comma changed the entire meaning of the sentence, and was therefore altogether different from the statutory version. The extra comma eliminated Talley's defense by suggesting that Talley could use no force whatsoever in self-defense unless the victim threatened him with deadly force. Furthermore, if the victim had threatened nondeadly force, according to the instruction, Talley would have had the duty to retreat, which is also inconsistent with the statute. Under this mistaken instruction, the jury could have believed Talley's version of events and still found him guilty, thus requiring a new trial.

The Florida Postconviction Journal

page 2 of 10   a quarterly publication of Loren Rhoton, P.A.

About Loren Rhoton, P.A.

Loren Rhoton, P.A. is a law firm that focuses exclusively on postconviction actions and inmate issues. The mission of Loren Rhoton, P.A. is to ensure that justice is accomplished in each and every case the firm undertakes. The firm's area of practice ranges from direct criminal appeals and postconviction actions to assisting inmates in dealing with the Florida Department of Corrections. Loren Rhoton, P.A., is a small firm, consisting of Mr. Loren D. Rhoton and Mr. Ryan J. Sydejko. The firm strives to keep a small caseload in order to give each case the individual attention it deserves. We are not a volume business. We do not accept every case that is presented to the firm for representation. A thorough review of any potential case will be conducted before the firm undertakes full representation. If you wish to have your case reviewed for representation, please contact Loren Rhoton for more information. If inquiring about representation, please do not send any materials to the firm that you wish to have returned to you.

Loren D. Rhoton, Esq.

Loren D. Rhoton is an attorney in private practice with the law office of Loren Rhoton, P.A., in Tampa, Florida. Mr. Rhoton graduated from the University of Toledo College of Law and has been a member in good standing with The Florida Bar since his admission to practice in 1995. The exclusive focus of Mr. Rhoton's practice is dedicated to assisting Florida inmates with their criminal appeal/postconviction cases.

Mr. Rhoton is a member of The Florida Bar's Appellate Division. He is also a member of the U.S. District Court, in and for the Southern, Middle and Northern Districts of Florida. Mr. Rhoton is licensed to practice before the U.S. Court of Appeals for the 11th Circuit and is also certified to practice before the U.S. Supreme Court. Mr. Rhoton regularly practices before Federal District Courts and the U.S. Court of Appeals for the 11th Circuit.

Mr. Rhoton typically deals with clients who have lengthy prison sentences. Mr. Rhoton has investigated and pursued hundreds of postconviction cases. He has practiced in all phases of the Florida Judicial System, all the way from misdemeanor county courts up to the Florida Supreme Court. Additionally, Mr. Rhoton has been directly responsible for amendments to Florida Rule of Criminal Procedure 3.850 (the main vehicle for most postconviction actions). Mr. Rhoton was appointed by the Florida Supreme Court to the Florida Criminal Rules Steering Committee, Subcommittee on Postconviction Relief, which focused on rewriting Florida Rule of Criminal Procedure 3.850. Mr. Rhoton worked on said subcommittee with judges and other governmental officials in an effort to improve the administration and execution of postconviction proceedings. Mr. Rhoton's role on said committee was to advocate for changes that were beneficial to postconviction litigants.

For over a decade, Mr. Rhoton authored a bimonthly article, *Post Conviction Corner*, for Florida Prison Legal Perspectives. Selected articles from *Post Conviction Corner* have been compiled and printed in a legal self-help book, *Postconviction Relief for the Florida Prisoner*. Mr. Rhoton also served on the Board of Directors of the Florida Prisoners' Legal Aid Organization.

Ryan J. Sydejko, Esq.

Ryan J. Sydejko is an attorney with the law office of Loren Rhoton, P.A. His practice focuses primarily on postconviction matters for those incarcerated throughout the State of Florida. He has argued cases before many circuit courts and District Courts of Appeal and has several published opinions. Mr. Sydejko has also presented cases to the Supreme Court of Florida and the U.S. District Courts for the Middle and Northern Districts of Florida.

Mr. Sydejko graduated from the University of Minnesota with a degree in political science and attended the University of Tulsa College of Law. As a student, he authored a law review article entitled: "International Influence on Democracy: How Terrorism Exploited a Deteriorating Fourth Amendment." The article, exploring how domestic terrorist threats have reshaped everyday law enforcement procedures, was published in the Spring 2006 edition of the Wayne State University Law School Journal of Law in Society. Mr. Sydejko also wrote articles for the Florida Prison Legal Perspectives. Mr. Sydejko is a member in good standing with the Florida Bar and is qualified to practice in all Florida state courts, as well as the Federal District Courts for the Middle and Northern Districts of Florida.

The Florida Postconviction Journal

Volume 2
Issue 3

a quarterly publication of Loren Rhoton, P.A.

page 3 of 10

Notable Firm Cases

Dames v. State, 773 So.2d 563 (Fla. 2d DCA 2000) – Improper summary denial of Rule 3.850 Motion reversed & remanded for evidentiary hearing.

Dames v. State, 807 So.2d 756 (Fla. 2d DCA 2002) – First Degree Murder conviction vacated & new trial granted due to ineffective counsel

Battle v. State, 710 So.2d 628 (Fla. 2d DCA 1998) – Improper Habitual Felony Offender Sentence on violation of probation reversed & remanded for resentencing

Mitchell v. State, 734 So.2d 1067 (Fla. 1st DCA 1999) - counsel can render ineffective assistance for failure to argue boarded-up structure is not a 'dwelling' under arson statute

Caban v. State, 9 So.3d 50 (Fla. 5th DCA 2009) – counsel can be ineffective for failing to object to improper impeachment of defense expert witnesses in Shaken Baby Syndrome case

Graff v. State, 846 So.2d 582 (Fla. 2d DCA 2003) – attorney's misadvice as to potential sentence can amount to ineffective assistance of counsel sufficient to justify withdrawal of plea.

Easley v. State, 742 So.2d 463 (Fla. 2d DCA 1999) – counsel can render ineffective assistance for failure to investigate insanity defense.

Campbell v. State, 16 So.3d 316 (Fla. 2d DCA 2009) – Manifest Injustice – summary denial of Rule 3.800 motion to correct illegal sentence reversed & remanded on manifest injustice grounds.

Thompson v. State, 987 So.2d 727 (Fla. 4th DCA 2008) – Reversal of Life Sentences – entitled to *de novo* resentencing upon correction of improper consecutive life sentences for murder and burglary.

Williams v. State, 777 So.2d 947 (Fla. 2000) – Right to Belated Postconviction Motion – if post-conviction counsel fails to timely file Rule 3.850 Motion, defendant has right to file belated appeal.

Parker v. State, 977 So.2d 671 (Fla. 4th DCA 2008) – Sentence reversed & remanded for resentencing due to judicial vindictiveness.

When Mental Illness Leads Defendant to Mistakenly Exercise Self-Defense

In Martin v. State, 2013 WL 646231, the First DCA recently dealt with an issue related to a delirious defendant and his response to a police presence on the defendant's property.

In Martin, the sheriff's office was performing a welfare check on Martin after receiving a call. Deputies approached, and Martin responded by cussing at the deputies and retrieving his firearm. As deputies slowly retreated, Martin fired a shot into the air.

Martin called two doctors at trial. The first, a board certified psychiatrist, testified that Martin was experiencing temporary insanity caused by delirium. The second, a clinical psychologist, testified that Martin was experiencing paranoid delusions. Both agreed that their diagnoses supported a finding that Martin feared for his safety. The trial court prohibited the defense's attempt to elicit testimony from the experts that Martin's firing of the gun was attempt at self-defense. Additionally, the trial court denied the defense's requested jury instruction of self-defense. Martin was found guilty of aggravated assault on a law enforcement officer.

The First DCA began by noting that a defendant's fundamental right to present witnesses and offer evidence relevant to the defense, even if only indirectly establishing reasonable doubt. In this respect, the DCA found error in prohibiting the defense from presenting testimony regarding self-defense.

To compound the error, the DCA also found the trial court erred in denying the self-defense jury instruction. The DCA noted an entitlement to the jury instruction if "any" evidence supports the defense theory. Because both defense doctors testified that Martin was experiencing episodes of confusion, misperception, and a general feeling that others were out to harm him, the requested instruction was relevant to the defense at trial.

The State argued that the error was harmless. The DCA rejected this argument, finding that the denial of Martin's ability to raise a valid self-defense claim was not harmless in light of his belief that he was threatened and his belief that firing the gun was an act of self-defense.

To Order Back Issues of
The Florida Postconviction Journal:

Please send a check or money order made payable to Loren Rhoton, P.A. in the amount of $3.50 per issue. Also, please designate the Volume and Issue number of each issue desired (found on the first page of each issue). Allow two to three weeks for delivery.

a quarterly publication of Loren Rhoton, P.A.

Credit for Time-Served:
Probationary Split Sentences vs. True Split Sentences

by Ryan Sydejko

A seemingly endless source of confusion for defendants, lawyers, and judges alike, is in what situations credit for time served may be applied to a sentence. The Fifth District Court attempted to address this confusion recently in Mann v. State, 2013 WL 1234682 (Fla. 5th DCA 2013).

First, it is important to distinguish the two sentences. A "true" split sentence is one in which a total period of confinement is imposed with a portion of the confinement period suspended and the defendant placed on probation for that suspended portion. Poore v. State, 531 So.2d 161, 164 (Fla. 1988). Whereas, a "probationary" split sentence consists of a period of confinement, none of which is suspended, followed by a period of probation. Id. To the naked eye, the difference may seem like semantics. But there are very real differences.

For example, a court could impose a true split sentence by sentencing a defendant to 42-months incarceration with two-years suspended. Mann, 2013 WL 1234682. In practicality, the defendant would serve 18-months incarceration, and, assuming no violations, would serve the following 24-months on probation.

By contrast, a court could achieve a similar result via a probationary split sentence by imposing 18-months incarceration followed by 24 months' probation. Notice the lack of a 'suspended' portion of incarceration. Franklin v. State, 545 So.2d 851, 852 (Fla. 1989).

The difference is important for one significant reason: credit for time served. "A defendant sentenced to a probationary split sentence who violates probation and is resentenced to prison is entitled to credit for all time actually served in prison prior to his release on probation unless such credit is waived." Mann (citing Bradley v. State, 631 So.2d 1096 (Fla. 1994). Thus, in the example above, the hypothetical defendant given a probationary split sentence that violates probation could be sentenced to two-years imprisonment, but would be awarded 18-months credit for time served. Mann, 2013 WL 1234682. In the situation of a true split sentence, however, a trial court can revoke probation and impose either the suspended portion of incarceration or the original period of incarceration. Moore v. Stephens,

804 So.2d 575, 577 (Fla. 5th DCA 2002). Credit for time served is available only if the court re-imposes the original period of incarceration. Moore v. Stephens, 804 So.2d 575, 577 (Fla. 5th DCA 2002).

In the example above, the hypothetical defendant whom violated the true split sentence could either be sentenced to the original term of imprisonment (42-months) with credit for time served, or to only the suspended portion (24-months) with no credit for time served.

Obviously, the calculations play significantly to the defendant's favor with a probationary split sentence, which is what the defendant sought in Mann. In Mann, the court confusingly sentenced the defendant to 18-months incarceration, followed by "12-months probation, within that 12-months probation is a two year suspended sentence back at DOC." Id. When Mann violated probation, the court imposed incarceration of two-years (representing imprisonment for that originally suspended portion). Id. The District Court reversed, holding that Mann's sentence was not a 'true' split sentence because the court imposed a specific term of incarceration, followed by a specific term of probation. Remember, in a 'true' split, the court sentences a defendant to a term of incarceration, and suspends a portion of it. Thus, Mann was entitled to credit for the 18-months previously served on his new 24-month sentence.

Thus, it is important to carefully review the sentencing judge's language at sentencing to determine exactly what type of sentence was imposed. There are occasions, such as Mann's, where the trial judge intends one thing, but does another. This is especially true in situations, such as Mann's, where the sentence is arrived at pursuant to a negotiated plea as the judge's imposed sentence may differ significantly from that which a defendant thinks he has negotiated. While some of this language can be confusing, a quick read of Mann and Moore should help shed light on the sentence and allow a pro-se movant to determine whether any additional credits are available.

Florida Supreme Court Rejects DCA Attempts to Limit Montgomery Claims

Often, when caselaw helpful to criminal defendants is issued, the appellate courts rush to limit the application of said legal authority. This was definitely the case with Montgomery v. State, 39 So. 3d 252 (Fla. 2010), which held that the standard jury instruction for manslaughter was fundamental error because it required intent to cause death.

For example, the Second DCA has held that the giving of the erroneous manslaughter by act instruction was not fundamental error where the jury was also instructed on manslaughter by culpable negligence. Haygood v. State, 54 So.3d 1035 (Fla. 2nd DCA, 2011). The Fourth and Fifth DCAs also applied the Haygood Rule: Cary v. State, 84 So.3d 404 (Fla. 4th DCA, 2012); and Paul v. State, 63 So.3d 828 (Fla. 5th DCA 2011). However, in Haygood v. State, 38 F.L.W. S93 (Fla. 2013),the Florida Supreme Court has now rejected the Second DCA's Haygood Rule. In so doing, the Florida Supreme Court held that a trial court's jury instruction on manslaughter by culpable negligence does not cure the fundamental error in giving an erroneous manslaughter by act instruction where the defendant is convicted of second-degree murder and the evidence supports a finding of manslaughter by act, but does not reasonably support a finding that the death occurred due to the culpable negligence of the defendant.

Therefore, the Florida Supreme Court's decision potentially opens additional avenues of relief to inmates who were previously denied the ability to successfully argue a Montgomery claim

Support Services for Inmates & Their Families Available

If you have a suggestion for a group or inmate resource that should be listed in our newsletter, please contact us with the information and we will share any helpful information in future issues.

The Florida Postconviction Legal Aid Organization, Inc. – www.myfplp.org
P.O. Box 4104, Milton, FL 32572
Phone: (850) 400-1205; Email: myfplp@aol.com
***FPLAO publishes a newsletter for inmates called the Florida Postconviction Legal Perspectives (FPLP). The FPLP addresses issues of interest to Florida prisoners such as promoting accountability of corrections officials. To become a member and receive monthly FPLP newsletters, contact FPLAO as the address above. Subscriptions cost $18.00 for prisoners and $26.00 for family members/individuals. [The Florida Postconviction Journal is not affiliated with FPLAO or FPLP, and derives no funds from the subscription costs. We merely provide this information as a service to our readers. DO NOT SEND MONEY TO THE FLORIDA POSTCONVICTION JOURNAL FOR FPLAO MEMBERSHIP. ALL INQUIRIES ABOUT FPLAO MEMBERSHIP MUST BE ADDRESSED TO FPLAO'S ADDRESS ABOVE.

Florida Legal Services, Inc.
www.floridalegalhelp.org
2425 Torreya Dr.,   Tallahassee,
Phone: (850) 385-7900; Fax: (850) 385-9998
*Provides referrals in civil matters.

Prisontalk.com.   An Internet community/forum that provides general information and networking for families of inmates. Also, has Florida specific forum that addresses issues ranging from dealing with the D.O.C. to coping with incarceration.

Florida Justice Institute, Inc.
4320 Bank of America Tower
100 S.E. Second Street
Miami, FL, 33131
Phone: (305) 358-2081
Contact: Randall C. Berg, Jr.
Email: rcberg@floridajusticeinstitute.org
*Handles civil-rights cases regarding conditions in prisons and jails; advocates and lobbies on behalf of prisoners.

Innocence Project of Florida.
1100 East Park Ave.
Tallahassee, FL, 32301
Phone: (850) 561-6767
*Assists inmates with postconviction DNA innocence cases and helps exonerees in obtaining compensation for wrongful convictions.

To Subscribe or Change Your Mailing Address to *The Florida Postconviction Journal:*

The *Florida Postconviction Journal* is currently being provided, free of charge, to Florida inmates who are interested in receiving the helpful advice and information contained in the newsletter. If you wish to have your name added to the newsletter's mailing list, please fill out the form below and mail it to Loren Rhoton, P.A., 412 East Madison Street, Suite 1111, Tampa, FL 33062. For non-inmates interested in subscribing to the newsletter, please forward a money order in the amount of $25 for a one-year subscription.

Please Check One:

☐ New Subscriber

☐ Change of Address

Name   DC#

_____

Institution Name and Street Address

_____

City   State   Zip

Juror's Use of Cell Phone Results in New Trial

A new trial can be warranted if the jurors considered unauthorized materials affecting their verdict. <u>Bush v. State</u>, 809 So.2d 107 (Fla. 4th DCA 2002). And, juror misconduct gives rise to a rebuttable presumption of prejudice. <u>James v. State</u>, 843 So.2d 933, 937 (Fla. 4th DCA 200). In <u>Tapanes v. State</u>, 43 So.3d 159, 162 (Fla.4th DCA 2010), a juror used his cell phone to look up the definition of "prudent" and such use of a cell phone was found to be juror misconduct. The <u>Tapanes</u> Court found that using a phone to "access a dictionary is, of course, no different than utilizing a bound dictionary. A dictionary is not one of the materials permitted to be taken into the jury room." *See*, <u>Smith v. State</u>, 95 So.2d 525, 528 (Fla.1957); <u>Greenfield v. State</u>, 739 So.2d 1197 (Fla. 2nd DCA 1999). Thus, a dictionary cannot be considered by the jurors. The fact that the foreperson utilized the phone to look up the definition of the word during a break and later shared his recollection of the definition with other jurors during deliberations was no less a juror misconduct than if the foreperson physically brought the phone into the jury room and read the definition therefrom.

Once juror misconduct is established by juror interview, the moving party is entitled to a new trial *unless* the opposing party can demonstrate that there is no reasonable possibility that the juror misconduct affected the verdict." <u>Norman v. Gloria Farms, Inc.</u>, 668 So.2d 1016, 1020 (Fla. 4th DCA 1996). In <u>Tapanes</u>, looking up the definition of "prudent" was not irrelevant. The word "prudent" was mentioned in the jury instructions given by the trial court and the state mentioned the term repeatedly during closing argument. The facts of Tapanes's case centered on whether the appellant acted in a "prudent" manner by his actions when confronted by the victim at his front door and whether the appellant should have called 911 instead of opening the door. The concept of "prudence" could well have been the key to the jury's deliberations. At the very least, the court could not say that there was no reasonable possibility that the juror's misconduct, by utilizing the phone to retrieve the definition of "prudence," did not affect the verdict.

The results of <u>Tapanes</u> are consistent with that of other courts which, for many years, have reversed convictions for the improper utilization of dictionaries. *See* <u>Smith</u>, 95 So.2d at 528; <u>Grissinger v. Griffin</u>, 186 So.2d 58 (Fla. 4th DCA 1966); <u>Jordan v. Brantley</u>, 589 So.2d 680 (Ala.1991) (finding prejudice where foreperson used a dictionary to look up meaning of "prudent" and "reasonable" and discussed the meanings with other jurors); <u>Alvarez v. People</u>, 653 P.2d 1127, 1130-32 (Colo.1982) (finding prejudice where a juror looked up the words "reasonable," "imaginary," and "vague" and shared the definitions with another juror).

The Florida Postconviction Journal

Volume 2
Issue 3

a quarterly publication of Loren Rhoton, P.A.

Desperate Prosecutors and Improper Closing Arguments

The Fourth District Court of Appeal recently handed down opinions in three cases dealing with overly aggressive prosecutorial arguments.

In the first such case, Becker v. State, 2013 WL 811664, the DCA reversed a conviction for solicitation to commit home invasion robbery and ordered a new trial. The State's star witness, a fourteen-time convicted felon serving probation at the time of trial, testified as an informant against Becker. The defense relied entirely on this witness' lack of credibility as their defense. The witness testified that he was getting no favors from the State for his testimony. Yet, the defense showed on cross-examination that the witness had been arrested recently on two felonies, but somehow didn't spend a single day in prison, thus eluding that something was going on behind the scenes. In closing, the prosecutor argued: "I can stand here today, ladies and gentlemen, as an officer of this Court, and tell you that [the informant] is not getting anything out of this."

The Court, in no uncertain terms, held that the prosecutor's comments were improper bolstering and vouching. In effect, the prosecutor "offered extra-testimonial knowledge" invoking his status "as an officer of the court to assure the jury that the informant was being truthful." Ultimately, the Court found these comments to have "undermined the integrity of the judicial process and irreparably contaminated the verdict and resulting sentence."

In the second case, Garcia v. State, 2013 WL 811598, the DCA reversed a conviction of dealing in stolen property. Prior to her arrest, Garcia had given a statement to police. At trial, Garcia's defense focused on the involuntariness of that statement as a reason for the jury to disregard it. The State countered, however, arguing: "I assure you, you wouldn't be listening to that tape if they were not freely and voluntarily made. That is an argument by the defendant. I assure you that does not apply here."

The Court held, as the jury instructions stated, that a jury can disregard a confession if the jury believes it was involuntarily given. The State's argument incorrectly implied the voluntariness of Garcia's confession had been predetermined, warranting a new trial.

In the final case, Petruschke v. State, 2013 WL 811616, the DCA reversed two counts of lewd and lascivious molestation of a minor. During closing, the Court found the prosecutor to have made so many improper arguments that Petruschke was denied a fair trial. In closing, the prosecutor argued that the child-victim was so young as to have lacked the mental ability to lie and repeatedly referred to Petruschke as a pedophile. Both the bolstering and character attacks were "so egregious that [Petruschke] was deprived of a fair trial.

Open Plea that Violates Double Jeopardy Requires Resentencing

by Loren D. Rhoton

The 5th Amendment the U.S. Constitution provides, "No person shall ... be subject for the same offence to be twice put in jeopardy of life or limb." This provision, known as the Double Jeopardy Clause, encompasses four distinct prohibitions: subsequent prosecution after acquittal, subsequent prosecution after conviction, subsequent prosecution after certain mistrials, and multiple punishments in the same indictment. North Carolina v. Pearce, 395 U.S. 711, 717 (1969). Double jeopardy claims will typically be raised on direct appeal. However, they can also be raised in a Rule 3.850 postconviction motion. The focus of this article will be on collaterally attacking a guilty or nolo contendere plea when there are double jeopardy violations because of multiple punishments resulting from the same conduct.

A double jeopardy violation, in the context of this article, results when a defendant has multiple sentences arising out of a single criminal episode, and the elements for the multiple charges are identical. Where the same act or transaction constitutes a violation of two distinct statutory provisions, the test to be applied to determine whether there are two offenses or only one, is whether each provision requires proof of a fact which the other does not. Gavieres v. U.S., 220 U.S. 338, 342 (1911). If both offenses require the exact same elements, then there is a violation of the prohibition against double jeopardy. Blockburger v. U.S., 284 U.S. 299 (1932). But, a "single act may be an offense against two statutes; and if each statute requires proof of an additional fact which the other does not, an acquittal or conviction under either statute does not exempt the defendant from prosecution and punishment under the other." Blockberger at 304. In other words, if two criminal charges arise from a single criminal episode, and each charge requires an element of proof different from the other, then there is no double jeopardy violation. Some examples of double jeopardy violations include but are not limited to:

- Lewd and lascivious behavior with child, which arises out of single criminal episode when there is no significant spatial and/or temporal break in the episode. Cabanela v. State, 871 So.2d 279 (Fla. 3rd DCA 2004).
- Where a robbery conviction is enhanced because of use of firearm in committing the robbery, a single act involving use of the same firearm in the commission of the same robbery cannot form the basis of a separate conviction and sentence for use of firearm while committing the felony. Cleveland v. State, 587 So.2d 1145 (Fla. 1991).
- Where DUI manslaughter conviction was enhanced from a second-degree felony to a first-degree felony because defendant left the scene of the fatal accident, a separate conviction for leaving the scene of a fatal accident constitutes a double penalty. Ivey v. State, 47 So.3d 908, 911 (Fla.3rd DCA 2010).
- Resisting an officer with violence and resisting an officer without violence arose from a single criminal episode, and thus convictions for both offenses violated defendant's constitutional protection against double jeopardy. Williams v. State, 959 So.2d 790 (Fla. 2nd DCA 2007).
- Burglary of a dwelling with an assault or battery is subsumed by home-invasion robbery, such that convictions of both offenses arising from a single criminal episode violate the principles of double jeopardy. Davis v. State, 74 So.3d 1096, 1097 (Fla. 1st DCA 2011).

Sometimes a defendant will enter an open plea to charges and (for whatever reason) not realize that a conviction on several of the charges may amount to a violation of the protection against double jeopardy. Generally, a defendant who knowingly enters into plea bargain covering both charges and sentence waives any otherwise viable double jeopardy objection to the sentences. Novaton v. State, 634 So.2d 607 (Fla. 1994). But, in certain circumstances, such a plea that results in a double jeopardy violation can be attacked in a post conviction motion.

In Brown v. State, 1 So.3d 1231 (Fla. 2nd DCA 2009), the defendant entered an open guilty plea to four counts of robbery with a firearm, one count of carjacking, and one count of possession of cocaine. In a later 3.850 motion for postconviction relief, Brown contended that two of the robbery convictions involved only one taking from one victim during one criminal episode, thus amounting to a double jeopardy violation.

Brown held that a defendant may properly raise a double jeopardy claim in a 3.850 motion even after pleading guilty. See Coughlin v. State, 932 So.2d 1224, 1226 (Fla. 2d DCA 2006); Plowman v. State, 586 So.2d 454, 455 (Fla. 2d DCA 1991). This is so even though a

Open Plea (cont.)

guilty plea and adjudication of guilt generally precludes a later double jeopardy attack; an exception applies when the plea is a general or open plea, the double jeopardy is apparent from the face of the record, and there is nothing in the record to indicate a waiver of double jeopardy. Novaton v. State, 634 So.2d 607, 609 (Fla.1994); Demps v. State, 965 So.2d 1242, 1243 (Fla. 4th DCA 2007).

The Brown Court noted that a single taking from one cash register supports only one charge, and the presence of two employees does not transform one robbery into two. Lundy v. State, 614 So.2d 674 (Fla. 2d DCA 1993). It was held that the record in Brown did not support two separate robberies, and the double jeopardy violation was thus apparent from the record. Further, there was no indication in the record that Brown waived the double jeopardy claim.

The record attachments attached to the postconviction court's summary denial of the 3.850 failed to refute, and actually established Brown's double jeopardy claim. Accordingly, the Brown Court reversed the order denying Brown's motion for postconviction relief and remanded for the lower court to vacate the adjudication of guilt and sentence on the redundant count. It was ordered that Brown be resentenced pursuant to a corrected score sheet.

The Brown exception for collateral double jeopardy attacks is specific to open pleas where the double jeopardy violation is apparent on the face of the record and there was no waiver of the double jeopardy claim. The importance of Brown is in the relief that is required. Per Brown, a defendant can obtain a resentencing with the redundant double jeopardy charges omitted. This results in a resentencing pursuant to a corrected scoresheet, which omits the points for the duplicative counts, thus allowing for a lower minimum sentence score. Such a result is preferred where a defendant does not wish to actually withdraw the plea and take the case to trial (sometimes it is not wise to withdraw a plea and take the case to trial because the defendant will be subjected to a potentially harsher sentence).

A few words of warning are in order regarding a double jeopardy attack such as that addressed in Brown. A resentencing such as that in Brown should not result in a harsher sentence (and potentially can lead to a reduced sentence). Once a sentence has been imposed and the person begins to serve the sentence, that sentence may not later be increased without running afoul of double jeopardy principles; to do so is a clear violation of the Double Jeopardy Clause, which prohibits multiple punishment for the same offense. Ashley v. State, 850 So.2d 1265 (Fla. 2003). Despite the prohibition against a harsher sentence on the remaining count (after the redundant counts have been vacated), one should still guard against any possibility of vindictive sentencing. A defendant making a Brown claim should usually make sure that the original sentencing judge is still on the bench and ensure that the case is assigned to the original sentencing judge. Gay v. State, 898 So.2d 1203 (Fla. 2nd DCA 2005) [substitution of judges during post-conviction resentencing proceedings, with result that defendant was resentenced by judges other than the judge who originally sentenced him, without showing of necessity, constituted reversible error, especially where original sentencing judge was available]. It is important to ensure that the original judge is the judge for the resentencing in order to protect against a replacement judge wrongfully imposing a harsher sentence. If the original judge is involved in the resentencing, there is less chance of new sentence in excess of that which was already imposed because such a sentence would be deemed to be presumptively vindictive, and, thus subject to reversal. See, North Carolina v. Pearce, 395 U.S. 711 (1969) [where at behest of petitioner, state criminal conviction had been set aside, unexplained threefold increase in punishment in new sentence violated due process clause]. If a defendant is sentenced more harshly following appeal, then a presumption of vindictiveness arises which can only be overcome if reasons for harsher sentence affirmatively appear in the record and those reasons are based on objective information concerning identifiable conduct on the part of the defendant occurring after the time of the original sentence. Harris v. State, 653 So.2d 402 (Fla. 4th DCA1995). However, if a different judge is involved in the resentencing, and said judge imposes a harsher sentence, there is no presumption of vindictiveness, and the defendant must prove actual vindictiveness (which is much harder when there is no presumption of vindictiveness). Richardson v. State, 821 So.2d 428 (Fla. 5th DCA 2002). However, even with a new judge, the rationale of Ashley should still apply and it can still be argued that a harsher sentence is a violation of the protection against double jeopardy because of the increase in an already imposed sentence.

As mentioned above, Brown only applies to situations where there was an open plea and the double jeopardy violations were not waived and are apparent on the face of the record. Of course, double jeopardy issues can also be raised on direct appeal or in collateral attacks such as an ineffective assistance of counsel (trial or appellate counsel) claim. However, such claims are not the focus of this article and will likely be addressed in future issues of FPJ.

Loren Rhoton, P.A.

Postconviction Attorneys

412 East Madison Street
Suite 1111
Tampa, Florida 33602
Tel: 813-226-3138
Fax: 813-221-2182
Email:
lorenrhoton@rhotonpostconviction.com
rsydejko@rhotonpostconviction.com

- Direct Appeals
- Belated Appeals
- Rule 3.850 Motions
- Illegal Sentence Corrections
- Rule 9.141 Petitions
- Federal Habeas Corpus Petitions
- Clemency Petitions and Waivers

The Florida Postconviction Journal publishes up to four times per year. This Journal provides resources for information affecting prisoners, their families, friends, loved ones, and the general public of the State of Florida. Promoting skilled access to the court system for indigent prisoners is a primary goal of this publication. Due to the volume of mail that is received, not all correspondence can be returned. If you would like return of materials, please enclose a postage-paid and pre-addressed envelope. This publication is not meant to be a substitute for legal or other professional advice. The material addressed in the Journal should not be relied upon as authoritative and may not contain sufficient information to deal with specific legal issues.

The Florida Postconviction Journal
a publication of Loren Rhoton, P.A.
412 East Madison Street
Suite 1111
Tampa, FL 33602

CHANGE SERVICE REQUESTED

Name
Institution
Street Address
City, State, Zip

www.ingramcontent.com/pod-product-compliance
Lightning Source LLC
Chambersburg PA
CBHW051232200326
41519CB00025B/7348